A Prolegor

Evangelical 7

A Prolegomena to Evangelical Theology

Norman L. Geisler
Douglas E. Potter

Indian Trail, North Carolina

A Prolegomena To Evangelical Theology
© 2016 Norman L. Geisler

Published by Norm Geisler International Ministries | P.O. Box 2638 | Indian Trail, NC 28079 | USA
www.ngim.org

Printed in the United States of America

All rights reserved. No part of this publication may be reproduced, stored in a retrieval system, or transmitted in any form or by any means—electronic, mechanical, photocopying, recording, or otherwise—without the prior written permission of the publisher and copyright owner.

ISBN–13: 978-1536965131
ISBN–10: 1536965138

Scripture taken from the NEW AMERICAN STANDARD BIBLE® Copyright © 1960, 1962, 1963, 1968, 1971, 1972, 1973, 1975, 1977, 1995 by the Lockman Foundation. Used by Permission. (www.Lockman.org)

Contents

PREFACE ix
INTRODUCTION xi
SECTION ONE Introduction to Theology 1
  1 Theological Disciplines and Tools 3
SECTION TWO Metaphysics (GOD) 13
  2 What is Reality? 15
  3 What Do You Mean by "God"? 21
  4 What are the Arguments for Theism? 29
  5 Does the Christian God Exist? 41
  6 Are Miracles Real? 49
  7 What is Man that He Can Know? 57
SECTION THREE Epistemology (TRUTH) 65
  8 What is Truth? 67
  9 Is there a Correct Theory of Truth? 75
  10 How Do We Reason? 83
  11 Can We Talk About God? 91
  12 Is an Objective Interpretation Possible? 99
  13 Is History Knowable? 105
SECTION FOUR Theological Methodology 111
  14 How to Do Systematic Theology 113
APPENDIX: Faith and Reason 123
BIBLIOGRAPHY 127

Illustrations

Figure 1.1 Basic Divisions of Systematic Theology 4
Figure 1.2 Biblical and Systematic Theology Compared 5
Figure 1.3 Foundation of Systematic Theology 8
Figure 3.1 World Views. 28
Figure 4.1 Horizontal and Vertical Cosmological Arguments 31
Figure 4.2 Fallacy of Composition 33
Figure 10.1 Deductive Syllogism 86
Figure 10.2 Informal Fallacies 88
Figure 11.1 Analogical God–Talk. 96
Figure 11.2 Meaning & Language 97
Figure 12.1 Process of Knowing 102
Figure 14.1 Revelation: General and Special 114
Figure 14.2 Test for Canonicity. 115
Figure 14.3 Methodology 122
Figure A.1 Faith and Reason 125

PREFACE

This is a defense of evangelical theology for the beginning student. It certainly is also a primer for students already familiar with theology. Contained here–in is a glimpse into the classroom of the authors. This, as closely as possible, is a text of our lectures in Prolegomena. Each chapter covers a central topic or question related to the subject. Each chapter also contains educational aids such as objectives, questions and exercises, vocabulary words, and summaries to help the student master the material. Hence, it is intended to be used with or in preparation for classroom teaching, instruction and learning. This book, therefore, is a helpful resource to advance the educational and communication process between the teacher, student and subject matter.

Both authors are well qualified to introduce students to the study of this important and often neglected subject. Norman L. Geisler, Ph.D. has taught theology and apologetics in colleges and seminaries for over 60 years. He is the author of over one hundred books that include introductory as well as advanced works in Christian apologetics and theology.

Douglas E. Potter, D.Min. is an assistant professor and Director of the Doctor of Ministry program at Southern Evangelical Seminary. He has been teaching Christian theology for over a decade.

After studying this text and for a more advanced and comprehensive treatment of Prolegomena we encourage the reader to acquire Norman L. Geisler, *Systematic Theology,* and Thomas A. Howe, *Objectivity in Biblical Interpretation.*

INTRODUCTION

You might be wishing that we did not begin with such a foreign sounding word as **prolegomena** (*pro–leg–o–mena*). As with many theological terms, it is Greek in origin and means "that which comes before" or "before" (*pro*) "I speak" (*lego*). This is where we must start. Why? Could we just skip it? Why can't we just start doing theology? Some do, but this may be to their own theological peril. There are many things that come before we start to do theology. For example, we should see if it is possible or not to demonstrate that God exists? Why should we study about him if we cannot prove He exists? Furthermore, we should ask or want to know what kind of God exits and what He can and cannot do? Can He communicate with us? Does our language about Him really have meaning? If we say something is true about God, is it just a relative truth or absolute? These questions and many more make up the study of prolegomena. If we skip answers to these kinds of questions, we may find it much more difficult to reconcile some of our own thinking about God when we turn to the pages of the Bible.

Another way to look at prolegomena is to see it as a justification or defense for doing theology. Our attempt here is not to demonstrate the truth of the Christian faith. That is the task of

Christian *apologetics*.[1] Prolegomena assumes and relies on the conclusion that the apologetic task is successful. Instead, prolegomena is interested in justifying or defending a certain approach to theology. In that sense, it is the foundation to constructing a Christian theology or even its world view. For example, not all theologians or theologies agree. Some theologians, even some who consider themselves evangelicals, believe God changes. Such a movement among evangelicals has been termed open theism or neo–theism.[2] Other theologians believe the Bible is not inerrant or without errors. This has long been the position of liberal[3] and neo–orthodox theologians.

Evangelicals traditionally, however, affirm that God cannot change[4] and His word, inspired in original autographs of Scripture, must be inerrant (without err).[5] We could compare and contrast different theologies and methods, but how would we decide who is right? These differences, and the failure of even some evangelicals to affirm a correct view of God and Scripture, may be due to a failure in their prolegomena or a lack thereof. Hence, to make sure the God of one's philosophy agrees with the God of biblical Christianity, it is necessary to engage in prolegomena. Only this can serve to justify or defend evangelical theology. Some call it conservative, traditional, or even classical theology. Regardless of the name, we are asserting a philosophy and theology that supports the biblical view of God's nature and the inerrancy of God's word.

To accomplish this we inquire into four sections of study. The first, Introduction to Theology, introduces you to the disciplines

---

1. See Norman L. Geisler, *Christian Apologetics*, 2nd ed. (Grand Rapids: Baker Books, 2013) or for its educational role see my *Developing a Christian Apologetics Educational Program: In the Secondary School* (Eugene: Wipf & Stock, 2010).

2. Clark Pinnock, et al. *The Openness of God: A Biblical Challenge to the Traditional Understanding of God* (Downers Grove, InterVarsity Press, 1994). The term "neo–theism" as applied to this movement seems to go back to an essay by Clark Pinnock "The Need for a Scriptural, and therefore a Neo–Classical Theism" in *Perspectives on Evangelical Theology*, Kenneth S. Kantzer and Stanley N. Gundry, eds. (Grand Rapids: Baker Book House, 1979), 41.

3. Harold L. DeWolf, *The Case for Theology in Liberal Perspective* (Philadelphia: Westminster, 1959).

4. For a defense of the classical view of God see Norman L. Geisler, *Creating God in the Image of Man?* (Minneapolis: Bethany House, 1997).

5. For a defense of biblical inerrancy see Norman L. Geisler, ed. *Inerrancy* (Grand Rapids: Zondervan, 1980).

and tools available to do theological study. Following this we delve into Prolegomena covering three sections of study: Metaphysics (God); Epistemology (Truth); and Methodology (Theological Method). We deal with each area by answering questions and addressing problems that are raised which challenge, inform, and establish an evangelical approach to theology.

SECTION ONE
Introduction to Theology

So how do you introduce someone to theology? Thomas Aquinas once said that the principle function of his life was to speak about God (*Summa Contra Gentiles* I,2.2). What we think and say about God may very well be the most important thing about us. In building any structure, such as a house, there are various tools and materials available to use. Likewise, building one's theology also involves various tools and materials. Just as a foundation to a house, because everything else rests upon it, is extremely important; so also is the foundation of one's theology. Regardless of how beautiful and elaborate the superstructure may be, if the foundation is bad, or the tools and materials used to build it, are inadequate then it will collapse. Similarly, the theologian must have the proper tools and materials and know how to use them in order to build a theology on a secure foundation.

In this section we discuss the nature, subjects, and tools available to do theology (chapter 1).

1 Theological Disciplines and Tools

Objectives:
1. Distinguish between the different disciplines of theology.
2. Define each major division of systematic theology in order.

Theological Disciplines

As we will see, there are different disciplines or subjects of theology each with their own methods. Let's begin with a dissection of some key words. The word *theology* comes from a combination of two Greek words 1) *theos* which means "God" and 2) *logos* that means "word." Literally it is a word or discussion about God. Eventually this discourse is written down and/or taught to others. Hence the term *doctrine* or even *sacred doctrine* is used to indicate this teaching. If systematic, another Greek word that comes from the verb *sunistano,* it means to organize or stand together. Hence, systematic theology is the organizing of all truth about God. It is more than just a study of the Scriptures. It includes truth discovered about God from any other source. In the medieval period, Thomas Aquinas convincingly argued that sacred doctrine (or systematic theology) is the highest of all the sciences (or subjects) to be studied since it is the most comprehensive, taking from all others and having as its object of study God and His revelation.[1] Lewis Sperry Chafer (1871–1952), a systematic theologian wrote in his multi volume work that systematic theology may be defined as "the collecting, scientifically arranging, comparing, exhibiting, and defending of all facts from any and every source concerning God and His works."[2] A more recent systematic theology by Norman L. Geisler says, "Systematic Theology is an attempt to construct a comprehensive and consistent whole out of all revelation from God, whether special (biblical) or general (nature) revelation."[3] Unlike other theologies we will look at, systematic theology which covers all of God's revelation found in the Bible known as special revelation and revelation found in nature which is known as general revelation. Since God is the author and creator of both special and general revelation, we can confidently approach both venues to discover truth about God. Using reason to discovering truth about God apart from Scripture is sometimes called natural theology. This does not mean that there aren't difficulties or problems to solve. But it does mean that ultimately what God says (inspired through human prophets), and what God does (creates the universe) must agree.

1. Prolegomena (Introduction)
2. Bibliology (*biblios*)
3. Theology Proper (*Theos*)
4. Christology (*christos*)
5. Hamartiology (*harmartia*)
6. Soteriology (*soterios*)
7. Ecclesiology (*ecclesia*)
8. Eschatology (*eschatos*)

Figure 1.1
Basic Divisions of Systematic Theology

There are eight main divisions of subjects and some subdivisions of systematic theology as follows: 1) Prolegomena, is a subject that covers preconditions for doing theology. 2) Bibliology (*biblios*) studies the Bible particularly its human origin and divine inspiration. 3) Theology Proper (*Theos*) studies God's existence, nature, and creation. There are subdivisions under this area that may take on large subjects of their own. They include 3a) Pneu-

---

1. Thomas Aquinas, *Summa Theologica* 1a.1.
2. Lewis S. Chafer, *Systematic Theology,* Vol. 1 Abridged Edition, John F. Walvoord ed. (Wheaton: Victor Books), 39.
3. Norman L. Geisler, *Introduction Bible*, Vol. 1 *Systematic Theology* (Minneapolis, Bethany House, 2002), 16.

matology (*pneuma*) which studies the Holy Spirit. 3b) Angelology (*angelos*) the study of angels. 3c) Satanology and Demonology (*daimonion*) the study of Satan and demons; and 3d) Anthropology (*anthropos*) the study of humans. The next major division is 4) Christology (*christos*) studies the divinity and work of Jesus Christ. 5) Hamartiology (*harmartia*) studies sin. 6) Soteriology (*soterios*) studies salvation. 7) Ecclesiology (*ecclesia*) studies the church. And 8) Eschatology (*eschatos*) studies last things.

Systematic theology has several benefits. First, it organizes all doctrines *necessary* to Christianity. For example, you may read verses about creation in the Bible, but unless you study every verse related to creation you would not have studied everything the Bible has to say about it. Furthermore, even if you did study every verse you will not know all the truth about creation, because there are some things to learn about creation outside the Bible from the field of science (general revelation). Second, systematic theology helps to enable a defense (apologetic) of Christian beliefs (1 Pet. 3:15). Apologetics provides reason and evidence to show that Christianity is true, but systematic theology demonstrates what the true Christian belief is that apologetics supports. Third, systematic theology is essential for the maturity of a believer (2 Tim. 3:16–17). Many Christians may not grow into maturity in their personal faith until they study theology. Only systematic theology gives a comprehensive view, for example, of the work of the Holy Spirit in their lives. Finally, it can protect the believer from error and heretical views (1 John 4:1, 6; Jude 4). Systematic theology not only studies the truth, but it also studies what is not true. In short, by studying systematic theology you can gain a comprehensive understanding of the Christian world view.

	Biblical Theology	Systematic Theology
Source	Special Revelation (Bible)	Special and General Revelation (Bible & Nature)
Examination	Individual Parts	Collective Whole
Results	Theology of Writer or Period	Theology of all Revelation
Method/ Approach	Exegetical & Historical	Philosophical & Inferential

Figure 1.2 Biblical and Systematic Theology Compared

In contrast to systematic theology, biblical theology studies a particular writer or era in Scripture to understand how theology developed. Charles C. Ryrie, in his biblical theology, describes it as "that branch of theological science which deals systematically with the historically conditioned progress of the self–revelation of God as deposited in the Bible."[4] Biblical theology examines the individual parts of Scripture, while systematic theology examines the entirety of Scripture. The resulting products are also different. Biblical theology produces a theology that is particular to a writer or period of time. While systematic theology produces a theology that comprehensively expresses the revelation (special and general) of God. The method of biblical theology is more narrow in that it involves exegetical (explaining the Scriptures) and historical (specific writer or period). Systematic theology is broader in that it encompasses truth found in other disciplines that may influence theology such as philosophy and the sciences.

Biblical theology covers the Old and New Testament and its disciplines may be divided as follows: Old Testament—Edenic Era, Noahic Era, Patriarchal Era, Mosaic Era, Monarchical Era, Prophetic Era. New Testament—Synoptics, Acts, James, Paul, Hebrews, Peter, Jude, and John.

Historical theology, you might have assumed, studies the doctrines of the Christian religion as they progressively developed through the centuries by different groups and people since the end of the apostolic era. It takes up where biblical theology leaves off. One historian describes it as "the history of Christian thought . . . drawing attention to the great achievements of Christian thinkers and stressing their formative role in intellectual history."[5] Charles Ryrie suggests that "historical theology focuses on what those who studied the Bible thought about its teachings either individual or collectively as in the pronouncements of church councils. It showed how the church has formulated both truth and error . . . ."[6] There are usually two basic approaches to historical theologies. The first

---

4. Charles C. Ryrie, *Biblical Theology of the New Testament* (Chicago: Moody Press, 1959), 12.

5. Geoffrey W. Bromiley, *Historical Theology: An Introduction* (Grand Rapids: Eerdmans, 1978), xxiv.

6. Charles C. Ryrie, *Basic Theology* (Chicago: Moody Press, 1999), 13–14.

is to divide it by historical periods: 1) Ancient Theology, 2) Medieval Theology, 3) Reformation Theology, and 4) Modern Theology. The second is to divide it by theological subject, such as those listed under systematic theology. This approach would study historically what was said, for example, about Theology Proper (God and creation), or Christology (Jesus Christ), etc.

Dogmatic Theology is more specifically applied to the study of a particular theology related to a denomination or person. It is dogmatic because the person or group believes it to be a true understanding of the Bible or theological tradition. Please note however, that this use of dogmatic theology is not followed by German and some other European theological works. Dogmatics in this context is the same as the American Systematic or Christian Theology. Examples of dogmatic theology are numerous but at least include the following major divisions: 1) Calvinistic Theology, 2) Arminian Theology, 3) Covenant Theology, 4) Dispensational Theology, 5) Roman Catholic Theology, and 6) Eastern Orthodox Theology. To a certain extent we could just have listed any particular denomination that has historically and formally expressed its theology.

Another discipline investigates some of the current trends or movements in theology. This is known as contemporary theology. Some of these may overlap with historical or dogmatic studies, but they are usually considered in the light of what recent theologians express in writing. Some of these disciplines include: 1) Liberal Theology, 2) Neo–Orthodox Theology, 3) Radical Theologies, 4) Historicist Theologies, 5) Socialist Theologies, 6) Catholic Theology, 7) Liberation Theology, and 8) Evangelical Theology.

The final subject of theology concerns the integration of theology into ministerial practices. Practical Theology studies theology to relate biblical truths to contemporary people for the purpose of ministry. Many fields of study use the results or products of various theologies from varying perspectives. These include the theology of Missions, Pastoral, Church, Evangelism, Counseling, and many others.

There are several other areas of study that are worth mentioning since they contribute to and support the study of theology. The first area, we have already mentioned is, *apologetics* (*apologia*) which means "to offer a defense." This studies the methods and

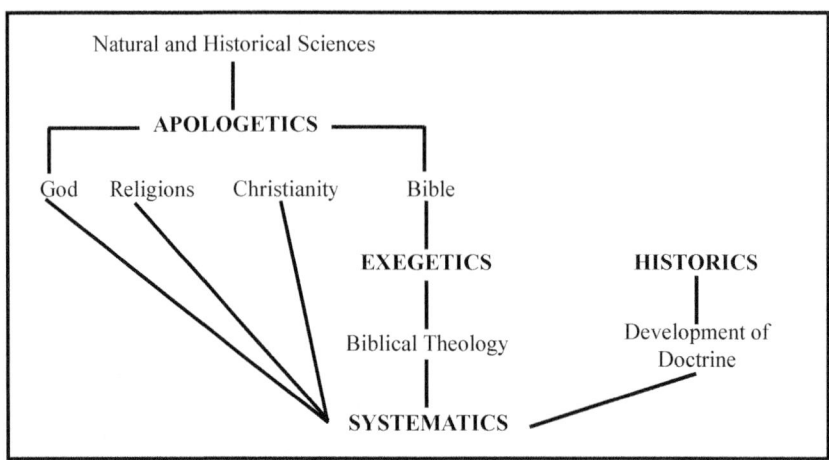

Figure 1.3 Foundation of Systematic Theology

body of knowledge (i.e., science) used to defend the Christian faith. Apologetics is best thought of as a foundation to theology, since it is given the task of demonstrating the truth of the Christian faith. Benjamin B. Warfield (1851–1921) gave an excellent chart to his students of theology to demonstrate not only the foundational nature of apologetics but the relationship other theologies have towards systematic theology (see Figure 1.3).[7]

A related area to apologetics is *polemics* which offers a defense of Christianity from internal doctrinal threats such as heresy and aberrant teachings. A study of church history demonstrates that theology is often formulated as a result of heresies that threaten the correct understanding of scriptural teaching. Finally *hermeneutics* and the practice of *exegesis* are essential to theology. The latter studies the science, skill, and art of interpreting the Bible and the former means to explain or interpret. The value of the work is often discovered by how well the interpreter is able to hold to the literal–grammatical–historical–method. This is the method that examines the type of literature (genre), its grammatical structure, and historical background to arrive at an objective meaning for a given text.

---

7. Benjamin B. Warfield., *The Idea of Systematic Theology*, Vol. 9, *The Works of Benjamin B. Warfield*. (Oxford 1932; reprint, Grand Rapids: Baker Books, 2003), 74. (page citation is from the reprint edition).

Theological Tools and Publications

From the above areas of theological study, you can imagine there must be several different kinds of published works and tools used for theological study. To begin our survey of these it is important to distinguish between a primary and secondary source as it relates to theology. The primary source for theological study is the Bible (Old and New Testament). The Old Testament was originally written in Hebrew and some in Aramaic. The New Testament was written in Koine Greek. There are many existing handwritten copies of each testament (or portions) which are called manuscripts. These are collected and examined to discover as closely as possible the original text. Secondary sources are other works that contribute to an understanding of the primary texts. For example, the *Novum Testamentum Graece*, Nestle–Aland Greek New Testament or the *Biblia Hebraica Stuttgartensia* would be considered a primary source, while a commentary on the biblical text would be considered a secondary source. However, the term "primary source" may also be used in reference to other ancient or even medieval works. For example, the early church fathers consist of three series of multi–volume works: 1) The Ante–Nicene Fathers, 10 vols. 2) Early Church Fathers: Nicene and Post–Nicene Fathers Series 1, 14 Vols. 3) Early Church Fathers: Nicene and Post–Nicene Fathers Series 2, 14 Vols. These primary sources may or may not be in the original language.

There are many different kinds of secondary sources to help the theologian understand the Bible. We begin with an order that one may consult to do research in areas of theological study, from specific works to more specialized and general works. The first is a Lexicon of the original language. This is a total inventory of words and their possible contextual meanings and usages. A work on semantic domains in various literature during the historical period helps with word usage. Next is a Dictionary or Encyclopedia. These usually consist of commentaries or articles written on words and topics. They can be general in nature such as a dictionary of a particular theology, biblical studies, or historical. They can also be more specific such as dictionary of the Old or New Testament, Paul, the Gospels or even subjects such as Apologetics, Missions, etc. Other specific works include theological and biblical journals.

Many higher academic institutions as well as ministries produce their own journals. Similar to this, higher educational theological students in some degree programs are required to write a thesis (master's level) and dissertations (doctoral level). These kinds of works can be very specialized, but they are usually not widely published or distributed. Titles and some abstracts of these works are usually available in theological libraries or on the internet.

Professionally published works are usually general in nature and correspond to the different subjects. For example Introductions to the Bible consist of General Introductions which deal with the inspiration, canonization, and transmission, and lower (textual) criticism. Special Introductions concern the authorship, date, addresses, occasions, and purposes for writing a biblical book. This is known as higher (historical) criticism. Commentaries on biblical books can cover individual books (Matthew, James, etc.), authors (e.g., Pauline, Johannine, etc.) or even historical periods.

Following these are the published works in the discipline of theology. These include systematic theologies (single or multi volumes). Biblical theologies can cover the entire Bible or just the Old or New Testament. Historical theologies can cover the entire subject or persons (e.g., a church father or theologian), periods (Patristic, Medieval, etc.), or doctrines (e.g., Trinity, Christology, Soteriology). Dogmatic Theologies can cover multiple dogmas or specific ones such as Dispensational or Covenant. Practical theologies may cover missions, pastoral counseling, family ministries, etc. Individual subjects or even specialized theological topics may have an entire text devoted to their study as well. These may include all the subjects of systematic theology and their related and foundational areas.

Systematic theology stands above other approaches to theology because it combines general and special revelation. However, to be complete systematic theology must rely on the work of other theological approaches, disciplines, and the various tools available.

Questions to Answer
1. What are the disciplines of theology?
2. Use a theological library or the internet to locate books that fit the following classifications: systematic theology (multi

and single volume), biblical theology, historical theology, dogmatic theology, practical theology, Anti–Nicene Church Fathers, theological journal, dissertation or thesis.

Terms and Concepts to know:
Prolegomena
Sacred Doctrine
Systematic Theology
Bibliology
Theology Proper
Christology
Hamartiology
Soteriology
Ecclesiology
Eschatology
Biblical Theology
Dogmatic Theology
Apologetics
Polemics
Historical Theology
Practical Theology
Contemporary Theology
Hermeneutics
Exegesis

Select Readings
Barber, Cyril J. & Robert M. Krauss. *An Introduction to Theological Research.*
Enns, Paul. *The Moody Handbook of Theology.*

SECTION TWO
Metaphysics (GOD)

Metaphysics is the area of philosophy that studies what is real ultimate or beyond the sensible. It literally means that which is beyond or after the physical. Sometimes it is divided into ontology and cosmology: The former deals with questions of being (*ontos*) while the later deals with questions about the origin of the universe (*cosmos*). It answers such questions as what is real? What does it mean to be real? Is reality one or many? And does God exist? In the tradition of Aristotle and Thomas Aquinas it is the study of being as being (what exists or can exist).

There are many preconditions to the study of theology in the area of metaphysics. We first consider the perennial challenge to theology from Monism (chapter 2) that presents the idea that everything is one. Second, we will consider what is meant by the term "God" in different world views (chapter 3). Third, we consider what can rationally be known about the existence and nature of God (chapters 4 and 5). Fourth, we defend the supernatural or miraculous aspect of God's activity (chapter 6). Finally, we explore the nature and capacity of humans to know (chapter 7). All of these questions cover ground important to the defense of evangelical theology.

2 What is Reality?

Objectives
1. Describe the problem posed by Parmenides and the four proposed solutions.
2. Explain the different kinds of beings related to actuality and potentiality.

Is Everything One: The Problem of Monism?

Parmenides (b. 515 BC) was a Greek philosopher born in Elea (lower Italy). He was the first to state a challenge to the belief in any kind of god by arguing for Monism in the following way.[1] There can be only one thing in the universe. If there were two things in the universe they would have to differ in some way. But there are only two ways to differ. One is by being (something) and the other is by non–being (or nothing). It is impossible to differ by nothing because to differ by nothing is not to differ at all. It is also impossible to differ by something because being is the only thing that makes them identical, i.e., what all things have in common. Metaphysically there is no differences between things and no way

---
1. Parmenides work is titled "On Nature" and exists only in fragments.

for there to be two beings. Therefore, there is only one being and Monism is true. Parmenides' argument seems to be valid. To attack this argument a non–monist must show how things can differ by being or non–being.

There were four basic responses or alternatives suggested to escape Parmenides' argument. First there were those who said there were differences in non–being. Atomists, such as Democritus (460?–370? BC) and Leucippus (5th century BC), said that they differed in absolute non–being. They argued that atoms constituted reality and that they were indivisible. Atoms differ in that they are in different spaces filling a void or absolutely nothingness. The void is simply an empty container of nothingness. Thus, things can differ by absolute non–being. In response, Parmenides would say that differing in absolute non–being is differing in absolutely nothing. How can these atoms of reality really differ unless there is a real difference? Therefore, the Atomists have not really solved the dilemma; they have just miniaturized it.

Plato (427–327 BC) one of the greatest Greek philosophers, believed that there were many beings. He argued for a difference in non–being saying that they differ by relative non–being. For example, a pencil is identified because it differs from the wall and is not anything else. Relative to anything else the pencil is not everything else. It is relatively not that. This solution involves the principle of negation. A cat is not a dog. Tall things are not short things. This is not that *ad infinitum*. But this raises a problem. How does one know what to negate unless there is some positive understanding of the thing being eliminated? All negations imply a positive understanding. We know the pencil is not the wall because we have some positive understanding of what is a pencil. There must be an infinite number of negations to know anything. It would be impossible for a finite mind to know anything. Parmenides would respond that this does not really solve the dilemma. If there is no difference in their reality (being) then there is no actual difference. There must be a positive understanding of being in which there is no real difference.

Others respond to Parmenides by saying that there were differences in being. Aristotle (384–322 BC), another great Greek philosopher and pupil of Plato, believed that there were 47 or 55 different gods or beings (Unmoved Movers). These beings were simple which means they have no parts. Each differs from the other in that they are simply different in their being. Again this does not solve the dilemma. The problem is that if being is the thing everything has in common, then only one being can exist. Thus, you cannot have 47 or 55 different beings.

Thomas Aquinas' Answer

Thomas Aquinas (c. 1224/5–1274), a Christian medieval theologian, answered Parmenides' challenge by asserting that there were different kinds of being. He argues that a being can be complex. It can have both unity and diversity in itself. The problem with Parmenides' argument, according to Aquinas, is that it begs the question in assuming a univocal (i.e., there is only one) meaning of being. If beings can be similar or analogous then different kinds of being can share in being.

Aquinas argues for a similarity or an analogous meaning of being. To help clarify Aquinas' point, imagine taking a trip to your nearest forest and stopping to observe the first tree that you see. If you observe the tree long enough, you will notice some things about the tree. First, that it exists! This may be obvious but it is quite profound since there is nothing immediately evident that makes the tree exist verses not existing. Second, over time you will notice that the tree changes. It changes internally in that it moves itself, to grow taller, or changes color and can be changed externally in that it no longer exists as a tree if it is cut down. Third, you will also notice that the tree you are observing is not the same as other things. It is not the same as the large rock, the grass, or the water near by. If you even observe it closely enough, you will notice that it is even different than all the other trees. Aquinas insists that these observations reveal principles about being. He says being is composed of *existence* (that it is existing) and *essence* (what it is e.g., a tree). His term for something that exists is act or actuality (existence) and his term for the fact that it changes is potency (capacity to change). Thus, it is possible to have different kinds of being in terms of their essence and act and potence. Aquinas goes on to observe that everything that is composed of act and potency cannot account for its own existence. Why?

Contingent things (i.e., composed things of act/potency), need not exist or could go out of existence. If that is the case, then the fact that it *has* existence must mean that its existence is dependent on something else. If it were not, then it would always exist (i.e., not be contingent). For something to exist it must be either 1) caused by itself, 2) uncaused or 3) caused by another. There are no other options. We can cross off the first one caused by itself. Self causation (*causa sui*) is impossible. It would have to exist prior to itself to cause its own existence. Uncaused also must be crossed off our list. After all, we already know it exists. So therefore it must be caused by something else. But what about that something else; must it also be composed of act and potency. Maybe, but Aquinas would tell us that there must be something that exists that has no potency in order to account for a world filled with existing things that have act and potency. In other words, there must be something that is pure Act (*Actus Purus*), without any potency or capacity for change. Something that is uncaused, but able to account for all the things needing a cause.

Aquinas, following Aristotle, not only recognizes that composed things need an ultimate cause, but also sees that there are different kinds of causes to be distinguished that help explain all dependent things. There must first be an *efficient* or *agent cause* that is God. The agent cause is that *by* which something comes to be; that is that which actualizes a potential or brings something into being. Second, there is a *material cause* or arranged matter. The material cause is that *out* of which something comes to be. This is the underlying stuff or matter something is made out of. Third, there is the *formal cause* or function. The formal cause is that *of* which something comes to be. This is its exhibited structure related to its form. Lastly there is the final cause. The *final cause* is that for which something comes to be. This is its goal, end or purpose of a thing that ultimately directs it back to its efficient cause or God.

These causes or explanations are general applying to everything in the natural world and human made artifacts; including all their components and sub components down to the smallest created thing. Such an explanation indicates the goal or directedness exists in the natural world regardless if something knows it or is aware of its causes or not. The material and formal cause go together in the sense that matter cannot exist without form. The efficient cause goes together with final causality since the final cause cannot exist without a formal cause. The final cause is the end reason for the other causes which also entail the act/potency distinction.

Our tree, for example and each of its component parts is explainable in terms of its efficient cause (i.e., God) that makes it exist; its material cause being the location of its particles (i.e., wood, leaves and their components down to atomic particles). Its formal cause being treeness (i.e., that exhibits its form); and its final cause being the end reasons for which it exists such as its function in the natural world which ultimately directs it back to its efficient cause.

Hence, there must be something that is pure actuality with no potentiality. There can only be one Being that is pure Act. That is one Being where what it is (essence) and that it is (existence) are identical. Every other being *has* being and is composed of act and potency. Since there can be different kinds of beings (those composed of act/potency) there must also be one Being that *is* Being or pure actuality. Parmenides' dilemma is therefore avoided.

Parmenides was correct in refuting those that said the difference was in non–being. There is no difference in absolute non–being. There can only be a difference in being and that difference must be, as Aquinas responds, in kind (act and potency) of being. As we will see, this difference can be demonstrated in arguments for the existence of God that show He is eternal and necessary. It can also be demonstrated in the substantial and accidental change of humans. The other philosophers had no concept of this complexity in being. Thus, they had no correct answer to Parmenides.

Questions to Answer
1. Develop an outline of Parmenides' argument for Monism and each suggested solution.
2. Explain the flaws of Parmenides argument for Monism and the solution offered by Aquinas.
3. Use Aristotle's four causes to explain a) natural things: human heart, cat and b) human artifacts: a chair, air plane.

Terms and Concepts to know:
Metaphysics
Parmenides
Monism
Pluralist
Atomism
Plato
Aristotle
Thomas Aquinas
Univocal
Composed
Act
Potency
Pure Act
Efficient Cause
Material Cause
Formal Cause
Final Cause

Select Readings
Geisler, Norman L. *Thomas Aquinas: An Evangelical Appraisal*, chap. 7.
Feser, Edward. *Aquinas: A Beginner's Guide*.

3 What Do You Mean by "God"?

Objectives

1. Describe the concept of God as understood in each world view.
2. Critique each world view opposed to theism.

World Views

A world view is the way one understands and interprets everything around them. Fundamental to any world view is the answer to the question, "what do you mean by God?" It might surprise you that there are really only six separate answers to that question. Each answer therefore generates a separate world view: 1) Theism believes in an infinite God beyond the universe, 2) Deism believes God is beyond the universe but he is not active (i.e., intervening through supernatural works) in the world, 3) Atheism believes there is no God, 4) Pantheism believes God is everything, 5) Panentheism believes God is in the universe as a soul is in a body, 6) Finite godism believes god is in and beyond the universe but is limited, a corollary view is that there are many finite gods. This is called Polytheism and believes there is more than one finite god. All people have a view of God that places them in one of these categories. For the most part the views are mutually exclusive; hence only one view can be true. We will examine each world view in terms of its understanding of God, the world, miracles, humans, and ethics.

Theism. Theism believes that there is an infinite God who created the world. Most theists believe that God exists beyond and in our world, which was created *ex nihilo* (out of nothing). God can and does perform miracles, and he created man in his own image. Theists believe that man will be sustained by God forever and will be judged according to his works in this life. Theism holds to moral absolutes in the area of ethics, the dignity of humans, and an ultimate meaning for life.

Many non-theists counter theist's arguments for God's existence by insisting that there could be an infinite series of causes and that the cause of the universe need not be eternal. They also attack theist's ideas that seem to make this life unimportant and promote inhumane acts in the name of an absolute deity. However, theists respond that human freedom is the cause of evil, and God is only responsible for the fact of human freedom. Ultimately, they believe, God will defeat evil since he is all-powerful. Three individuals who represent theistic thought included Augustine of Hippo (354–430 AD), Thomas Aquinas (1225–1274), and C. S. Lewis (1898–1963).

Deism. Deism, similar to theism, says that there is an infinite God who created the world *ex nihilo*. But Deism eliminates God's activeness in the world by insisting that he does not supernaturally intervene in the world. This naturalistic view of the world insisting that there must be a creator or originator of the finite universe that operates by strict natural laws. The only revelation that God has toward man is the world itself. Since there is no other revelation given, humans should live by reason and ignorance becomes the primary reason for evil. Deists accept that some moral laws are absolute (right and wrong), but they disagree over what laws are absolute and culturally relative.

Several criticisms have been leveled against Deists because they accept the greatest miracles of all (i.e., creation) but reject God's capacity or willingness to do smaller ones seems inconsistent. Many Deists accept the arguments of naturalism against miracles, but this is incompatible with a God who is acknowledged to be like a loving Father; Who provides for and cares for His creation. Natural laws are recognized today as descriptions of what normally occurs, not prescriptions for what must occur. Many of the founders of our country were Deists such as Thomas Jefferson and Thomas Paine. Martin Gardner, while rejecting the outdated title of Deists, nonetheless espouses such a view.

Atheism. Atheism asserts that God or god's do not exist. Atheists believe that the idea of God simply has no correspondence. They hold either that the world is eternal or that there is no explanation for its cause which is *ex materia* (out of mater). Miracles are obviously impossible and all such claims are either mythical, a hoax, or have a natural explanation. Humans are completely material with no immaterial aspect or eternal destiny. Evil is real and the result of ignorance but morality is culturally relative. Atheists reject traditional theistic arguments and put forth their own arguments to counter belief in the existence of God. Atheists usually try to turn theist arguments around as a disproof for the existence of God.

Theists try to show that their arguments are valid and that atheists arguments fail on several accounts. Most damaging to the atheist's belief is that a finite cause must have an infinite cause because everything cannot be contingent. Everything cannot be contingent because every finite contingent being needs a cause that cannot be finite. Therefore, an infinite being must exist. Theists point out that chance is not enough to explain the origin of all things. An intelligent cause is needed because of the design and information found in living things. Theists believe the principle of causality (i.e., every changing thing needs a cause) is valid because to deny it means that nothing produced something. Most of the atheist's dis proofs for the existence of God fail because they self destruct, make wrong assumptions, or fail to do what they claim. Some representative of atheism included Friedrich Nietzsche (1844–1900), Ludwig Feuerbach (1804–1872), and Jean–Paul Sartre (1905–1980).

Pantheism. Pantheism believes that God is everything and everything is God. Creation is *ex Deo* (out of God). They generally believe God is impersonal, that God is the world and that the world emanates and exists out of God. Miracles, as understood by Theism, are impossible since God is not outside the world and thus able to impose or intervene. They believe a human's goal should be to unite with God. Morals for a pantheist are not absolute but relative. Evil, they believe, is an illusion and one should strive through meditation to go beyond good and evil to unite with God. Pantheism is consistent in that it tries to maintain a holistic view of all things. It also teaches that human limitations should not be ascribed to God.

Some criticisms of Pantheism include the self–defeating affirmation that "I am God." Any human must come to know this and by the pantheist's own definition God is absolute and changeless. But if God is absolute and changeless then "I" (as God) would already know I was God. God always knows that he is God if he is changeless and absolute as the pantheists believes. Furthermore, how can an impersonal God account for a being that is personal, asks personal questions, and makes personal distinctions? Other criticism includes the impossibility of distinguishing reality from fantasy. If evil is only an illusion then why are its effects so real and experienced for so long? Pantheists believe that God is beyond good and evil. But if this is so, then there is no basis for moral absolutes. Murder and rape are as justifiable as kindness and love. Finally, pantheists believe that God is unknowable and yet they use many words to describe that he is unknowable. This is clearly self–defeating. There are different types of Pantheism, such as absolute, emanational, developmental, modal, multilevel, and permeational. These differ in how they view God as being one with the world. The Hindu scriptures called the Vedanta and Zen Buddhism are examples of Pantheistic beliefs. Other representatives of this world view include D. T. Suzuki (1870–1966) and the New Age Movement.

Panentheism. God and the world are dependent upon each other. God inhabits the world similar to a soul that inhabits a body. They believe God is bi–polar with an actual and potential pole. God's potential pole is beyond the world and his actual pole is in the world. Potentially God is unchanging and eternal. His actuality, what he is at any moment, is changing, finite, and temporal. God's bipolar condition includes a personal (changing) and impersonal (unchanging) pole. The universe is *ex hules* or *ex Deo* a cycle of continuous creation out of preexisting material that is constantly in flux because its self–created creatures are constantly changing. Most panentheists believe miracles do not happen because of their contemporary scientific view of the world. Since God is the world, there is nothing outside of Him to interject a miracle. Man is finite and free but his eternal destiny only exists in the mind of God. Evil is ultimately a necessary aspect of God's nature and human ethics are considered relative.

Criticism of panentheism includes the contradictory notion that God is both finite and infinite, personal and impersonal. God is also considered a self–caused being in the sense that he causes his own change (i.e., becoming) to take place. How can God cause his own change without an unchanging being that anchors the changing being's existence? Along with this is the problem of how one can know what is true if everything is relative and changing. Panentheism believes that we become a new person each moment. This is not likely because something in the person must remain constant to which change could be measured. If there is nothing constant then there is no basis for change. If there is something constant, then the person is not entirely in a state of change. Finally, they believe that God is able to comprehend the entire universe at one time. But panentheists believe that God is limited to time and space. It is impossible for a being limited to time and space to comprehend all time and space in one moment. Panentheism is also known as process theology, bipolar theism, and neoclassical theism. Alfred North Whitehead (1861–1947), Charles Hartshorne (1897–2000), Schubert M. Ogden and John B. Cobb are individuals who have significantly contributed to this understanding of God.

Finite Godism. Finite Godism believes god is powerful but is limited and imperfect. They reason that since the universe is finite and imperfect, so is god. A limited god is beyond the world and created it, but because of his imperfection, he cannot completely control it. Creation by god is out of pre–existing matter (*ex materia*) which may or may not be eternal. Humans may or may not have a soul that survives death, but they are generally viewed as a result of evolutionary processes. Miracles, in the all–powerful sense, are not possible. Morality also varies between absolute and relative, since god may or may not be able to control evil or establish a system of absolute right and wrong. Polytheism multiplies the number of existing finite gods and Henotheism establishes one god as superior. Eastern religions such as Hinduism and ancient religious of Greece and Rome have espoused this idea as well as the recent beliefs of Mormonism.

The obvious criticism of this view is that any finite god or gods needs a cause. Multiplying finite gods (polytheism) only stretches out the problem of causation. God is not the ultimate and cannot explain his own finite existence. Any finite god or god(s) is not worthy of worship since he is not ultimate. Furthermore, the universe eternal or not, presents a serious problem to a finite view of god. If eternal, then one must reject the discoveries of modern scientific evidence for a beginning of the universe. If the universe is not eternal then something other than the universe must exist to account for its existence. Either way a finite god(s) does not seem significant. Many individuals have held this view, including Plato, but few religions have sprung from it. William James (1842–1910), Peter Bertocci, and Harold Kushner represent some that hold the view that god is finite.

In addition to their internal inconsistencies, there is a significant philosophical problem to clarify and lay before the views opposed to theism. Remember our previous discussion (chapter 2) regarding act and potency. Aquinas said there are principles of being that apply to all finite changing things. Because of that, there must be a cause of all beings that account for all things that exist and change. That cause must itself be pure Act (existence) with no potential to change. It also must be the cause of things that have existence right now, since they exist right now. None of the world views, except Theism, is able to account for this observation of reality. Deism asserts that God does not intervene (or cause things supernaturally to be right now) in the world.[1] Atheism asserts there is no cause of things. Pantheism says the things of this world are self–caused (since they are God). Panentheism says the cause of things is an eternal being that also changes. And Finite Godism says the cause itself is finite and changing. Only theism rightly

---

1. Admittedly not all Deists would fall under this criticism, but we will address more fully the question of God's intervention (miracles) in chapter 5.

concludes that the cause of all finite changing things now must be pure transcendent existence, with no potentiality.

All approaches to the understanding of God opposed to theism are unable to completely explain or account for reality, make self-defeating claims or suffer internal inconsistencies. Only theism, as we explore next, is able to be justified through rational argumentation.

Questions to Answer
1. Draw a blank chart for each view of God similar Figure 3.1 on the next page and fill it in by memory.
2. Explain the philosophical problems in each world view opposed to Theism.

Terms and Concepts to know:
Theism
Deism
Finite Godism
Panentheism
Pantheism
Ex nihilo
Miracle
Self caused
Uncaused
Natural law
Ex Deo
Bipolar theism
Ex Materia

Select Readings
Geisler, Norman L. & William Watkins. *Worlds Apart.*
Geisler, Norman L. *Creating God in the Image of Man?*

28 A Prolegomena to Evangelical Theology

	Theism	Deism	Atheism	Pantheism	Panentheism	Finite Godism
God	One Infinite, personal	One Infinite, personal	No God	One Infinite impersonal	One potential infinite, actually finite, personal	One or many, finite personal
Miracles	Possible, Actual	Not Actual	Impossible	Impossible	Impossible	Not Actual
Creation	Ex nihilo	Ex nihilo	Ex materia	Ex Deo	Ex hules	Ex materia
Evil	Free choice, will be defeated	Free choice/ Ignorance	Ignorance	An illusion	Necessary aspect of God	God's struggle

Figure 3.1
World Views

4 What are the Arguments for Theism?

Objectives
1. Explain the different kinds of arguments for God.
2. Answer various objections to the existence of God.

Arguments for God's Existence

Natural theology is the subject that discover what can be known about God through nature by rational means. One task of natural theology is to see if it is possible to rationally demonstrate the existence of God. There are many arguments put forth for the existence of God. Before we consider some examples it is important to distinguish between proving and persuading. Arguments for God's existence should be offered to prove that God exists. Hence if an argument is valid and true then it stands as a proof for the existence of God. This is different than persuading someone that God exists. An argument may or may not do that for any number of reasons (i.e., psychological, moral, etc.). It is also important to realize that there are many ways, apart from formal rational argumentation, in which people come to believe in God.

They may have been brought up in a family, culture, or religion that asserts a form of theism. They may have an insight into the way the world is, and concluded that there must be a God. They may also simply accept it by faith (see Appendix). However, this fact does not negate the possibility of human reasoning concerning the existence of God. The many ways one may come to believe in God are not mutually exclusive. Since our goal, however, in this text is to justify a certain approach to theology, it is necessary and appropriate to demonstrate by rational means the existence of God.

Generally arguments for the existence of God can be classified in one of four types: Cosmological (*cosmos* meaning world), Teleological (*teleos* meaning design), Axiological (*axiom* meaning judgment), and Ontological (*ontos* meaning being). Such arguments are usually reducible to self–evident and undeniable first principles.[1] We will give examples of each and some of their major proponents, and conclude (in the next chapter) with one of the most forceful arguments for God's existence that also demonstrates that the God of our rational argument is also the God of the Bible.

Immanuel Kant (1724–1804) in his *Critique of Pure Reason* challenged these kinds of arguments for the existence of God by asserting agnosticism. This is the position that one cannot know (through argumentation) if God exists. While his assessment and views remain influential, even among some Christians concerning the value of these arguments, he has not demonstrated that all such arguments are invalid as we will show in the next chapter.[2]

The **cosmological** argument comes in two forms: horizontal and vertical (see Figure 4.1).[3] The **horizontal** form or **originating** cause was championed by Bonaventure (1224–1274) and Islamic scholars in the Middle Ages who called their theology Kalām. A contemporary Christian author who has renewed interest in this

---

1. For a list of these and their consequence see Norman L. Geisler, *Christian Apologetics*, 2nd ed. (Grand Rapids: Baker Books, 2013), 266–267.

2. See Stuart C. Hackett, *The Resurrection of Theism: Prolegomena to Christian Apology*, 2nd ed. (Grand Rapids: Baker Books, 1982). for an assessment of Kant's philosophy and attack on these kinds of arguments.

3. Adapted from Norman L. Geisler and Ronald M. Brooks, *When Skeptics Ask* (Grand Rapids: Baker Books, 1989), 19.

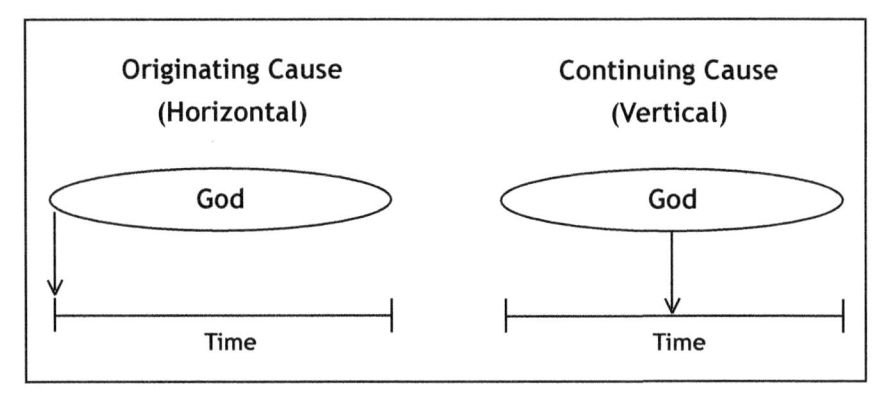

Originating Cause (Horizontal)	Continuing Cause (Vertical)
God → Time	God ↓ Time

Figure 4.1
Horizontal and Vertical Cosmological Arguments

argument is William Lane Craig.[4] It reasons:

1. Everything that begins to exist has a cause.
2. The universe began to exist.
3. Therefore, the universe has a cause.

The first premise relies on the undeniable principle of causality. Something that is an effect must have an adequate cause to explain its existence. Note it does **not** say everything must have a cause.

The second premise can be validated scientifically and philosophically. Scientific evidence strongly suggests that the universe had a beginning. The Inflationary Theory (i.e., Standard Model or Big Bang theory) states that at 10^{-34} seconds after the universe began all matter is condensed into a space of zero size and infinite density. But no object could be infinitely dense. If it contained any mass, it must be finitely dense. Such a contracted universe is really no universe at all. Hence, the universe must have begun from nothing (*Ex nihilo*). From this point on inflation (explosion from within) occurs. There are three main lines of evidence for this theory. The first includes Doppler shift in light emitted by galaxies. This is the evidence that the stars and galaxies are rapidly expanding away from each other and from a common center. Second, isotropic background radiation was predicted and confirmed to exist that gives evidence of an implosion that started the universe. This is similar

---

4. See William Lane Craig, *Reasonable Faith: Christian Truth and Apologetics*, 3rd ed. (Wheaton: Crossway Books, 2008), chapter 3 and William Lane Craig, *The Kalām Cosmological Argument* (New York: Macmillan, 1979).

to the smoke that fills a room after a gun is fired. Third, there is the 2nd law of thermodynamics as expressed in mathematical equations called entropy. This generalized law states that the amount of usable energy in a closed system, such as the universe, is decreasing. This indicates that the universe does not have an infinite amount of energy since it has not reached equilibrium (i.e., heat death), it must have a beginning.

A philosophical argument can also be made that supports the same conclusion. It is impossible to have an actual infinite series of events in time. For example, consider the possibility of an infinite number of books in the universe each being marked with a successive number. Would it be possible to add a new numbered book to this series? Not if all the numbers are used up (since it is infinite). But if they are real books it seems possible to take from the books a certain number of pages to create a new book to add to the set. This contradiction likewise exists with all objects of sensible reality since they can be numbered. While a mental or mathematical infinite set is conceivable, when the concept is applied to real objects in the space–time universe it is impossible. Therefore, an actual series of infinite events in time is not possible. If real time events were infinite, one could never add new time events or even arrive at the present time. Since, we are in the present an actual infinite is impossible.

One objection to this argument is that if an actual infinite is impossible, then God cannot be an actual or real infinite. However, this objection misses the point. God is the outside cause of all real temporal things that cannot be infinite. While God is real, he is not composed of temporal finite things which cannot be infinite. He is not a collection or set of things or beings, but one simple infinite being. Hence, our criticism of an actual temporal infinite series is not applicable to an infinite being such as God.

The conclusion, then, naturally follows: The universe must have had a beginning cause. While it may not seem, at first that the cause concluded from this argument is the Theistic God, it can be shown through further elaboration.[5]

The second form of the **cosmological** argument is called a

---

5. See Richard Glenn Howe, "An Analysis of William Lane Craig's Kalam Cosmological Argument" (master's thesis, University of Mississippi, 1990).

vertical or **continuing** cause. A form of it was made by Thomas Aquinas.[6] Norman L. Geisler has updated this argument for a contemporary reader as we will explain in the next chapter.[7] It reasons:

1. Finite changing things exist.
2. Finite, changing things must be caused to exist.
3. There cannot be an infinite regress of these causes.
4. Therefore there must be a first uncaused cause of every finite, changing thing that exists.

The first premise makes a claim about reality that is undeniable. To deny that finite (i.e., things that need not exist or could cease to exist) changing things exist is self defeating, since the existing person saying it, is finite and changing. Finite changing things cannot be self–caused (it would have to exist prior to existing) or uncaused (since they do exists), then they must be caused by another (Premise 2). An infinite regress of causes is impossible, since every cause is causing another. There must be a first uncaused cause. There must be a hook upon which to hang the chain of causes. So there must be a first uncaused cause of every finite, changing thing that exists right now.

One serious objection to this cosmological argument is the assertion that it commits the fallacy of composition. The fallacy of composition states that the whole does not necessarily have the characteristics of its parts. For example, Figure 4.2 is composed of two triangles but the whole figure is not a triangle. Likewise it is objected that just because the universe contains finite dependent things, does not entail that the whole universe is finite or dependent. However, there are many instances when the nature of composition of the parts does equal the whole. For example, a floor made of square tiles that are all green is a green floor. Likewise, combining geometric figures will always produce geometric shapes.

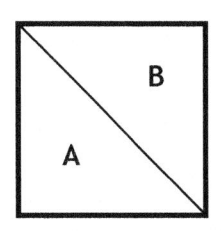

Figure 4.2
Fallacy of Composition

---

6. See Thomas Aquinas, *Summa Theologica* 1a.2.3
7. Norman L. Geisler and Winfried Corduan, *Philosophy of Religion*, 2nd ed. (Grand Rapids: Baker Books, 1988).

The nature of effects, as found in the universe, is that if you add them up they can only equal an effect: E + E + E + E = E. The same is true for dependant beings. If every dependent being in the universe ceased to exist would anything be left? If you answer yes, then one admits there is a non–dependent being (i.e., God). If No, then the whole universe goes away with no explanation for its dependent state of existence.

There are two kinds of **teleological** arguments. Aquinas' argument, also known as his Fifth Way, should be distinguished from that of Paley's (see below). Aquinas' makes a metaphysical argument that relies on the undeniability that things change or move from potentiality to actuality and in so doing tend towards a final end or purpose (see chapter 2). It may be stated as follows:

1. All unintelligent things directed towards an end must have an Intelligent cause.
2. Things (unintelligent) in the universe are directed towards specific ends.
3. Therefore, there must be an Intelligent cause.

All that needs to be shown is that some none intelligent thing is directed towards a specific end, purpose, or goal. This could be anything from a planet orbiting the Sun to an electron orbiting a nucleus. As long as it is unintelligent and directed towards a specific end as opposed to another there must be an intelligence to account for its final cause. If the physical universe consists of a system of such things, there must be some Intelligence outside the universe to account for this. Such Intelligence cannot be of the same causation or composition (act/potency) *ad infinitum* and therefore must be Intelligence that is pure Act. Such an argument does not rely on the design or complexity found in things, but upon their final cause and movement towards that end.

William Paley's (1743–1805) argument, reasons as follows:

1. All intelligent design requires a Designer.
2. There is intelligent design in the universe.
3. Therefore, there must be a Designer of the universe.

Much of the debate over this argument rests on what is meant by "design." While there may be natural formations found in nature that are called beautiful or even "designed," this argument rests on the point that some things found in nature cannot be the result of regular naturally occurring phenomena. It is the difference between simple and specified complex designs. Some designs give clear indication of an intelligence behind them because of their specified complexity. We would easily consider the Grand Canyon to be the result of natural occurring phenomena (wind, flood waters, etc.). But what would we say of the sculptures on Mount Rushmore? This is the kind of distinction being made in the first premise. The information content of DNA found in cells is quantifiable in terms of being equivalent to information[8] and some of the irreducible complexities at the molecular biological level clearly give evidence of intelligent design.[9] Because there is no conceivable way these systems could naturally evolve or function with certain parts removed, there must be a transcendent designer to account for their design.

The **axiological** or moral argument was made by William Sorley (1855–1935) and made popular by C. S. Lewis (1898–1963). It states:

1. All humans are conscious of an objective moral law.
2. Moral laws imply a moral Lawgiver.
3. Therefore, there must be a moral Lawgiver.

The first premise asserts that there are some moral principles that all humans are aware of. If all humans are aware of the same moral principles, then their origin cannot be within humans or their culture. Acts such as murder, genocide, rape, incest, etc. are always wrong everywhere in human culture to some degree. Even some virtues such as courage, love, etc. seem to be admired and others such as cowardice are shunned everywhere. Cultures have written codes to express moral laws which are common.[10] Often, however, they are most evident by the similar reaction people have when they are personally involved in a violation. You may think it is okay to steal someone's spouse, but what is your reaction when

---

8. Hubert Yockey, *Information Theory and Molecular Biology* (Cambridge: Cambridge University Press), 1992.

9. Michael J. Behe, *Darwin's Black Box: The Biochemical Challenge to Evolution* (New York: The Free Press, 1996).

10. A collection of similar moral codes from many different religions and cultures can be found in C. S. Lewis, *The Abolition of Man* (New York: MacMillan, 1947), Appendix.

someone steals your spouse? Your reaction to being wronged, reveals you believe there is a moral standard that makes some things right and other things wrong regardless of who you are or where you live. If this is the case, then there must be a standard that transcends human culture to account for this fact. Hence, there must be a supreme moral Lawgiver.

The **ontological** argument, developed by Anselm, states:
1. All perfections must be attributed to the most perfect Being (conceivable).
2. Necessary existence is a perfection.
3. Therefore, necessary existence must be attributed to the most perfect Being.

Most theists acknowledge that the ontological argument does have problems. In Kant's assessment of the ontological argument he observed that there is a difference in thinking about a ten dollar bill, and actually having one in your wallet. You can think about one as much as you want, but it will not mean you have a real one. Others have attempted to defend it against this criticism. Regardless of the arguments validity, as we will see, there is an important role the ontological argument has when it is combined with a cosmological argument. Because it does tell us some important things about a *definition* of what God must be like, if indeed he does exist.

You might be wondering at this point how all these arguments justify theology. They may help us conclude that God exists, but how do we know this God is the same God of the Bible? One way to do this is to combine all these arguments together, to discover what kind of God exists. For example, we learn from these arguments that God is all–powerful, eternal, all–good, and a necessary being. When we turn to the Scriptures we see that the same God of our argument must be the same God of Scripture (Heb. 1:2; Mal. 3:6; 1 Kings. 8:27; Ps. 86:5; Heb. 1:3). Since the God of our philosophy agrees with the God of the Bible they must be identical. There can be only one Being that is all–powerful, all–good, eternal, and necessary.

Objections to God's Existence

Arguments for God do not demonstrate the existence of the Christian God. This confuses what is known by natural theology versus what is only known via revealed theology. It is true that we cannot demonstrate by argumentation apart from Scripture the triune nature of God (i.e., the Trinity). This is only known by examining Scripture and is completely based on the authority of God's revelation. However, arguments for God and valid inferences made from those arguments can match the One infinite and eternal nature of God with the identical affirmation of the One divine infinite and eternal nature found in Scripture. As such, Parmenides argument when applied to the divine nature, as opposed to creation, stands true (chapter 1). There can be only one infinite and eternal being, so a philosophical argument for God and the God concluded from Scripture must be one and the same Being.

Why does the Bible describe God as changing if He does not change? The Bible as well as our common language used to speak about God is filled with metaphors and anthropomorphism (Gen. 6:6; Deut. 5:15; Job 11:6; 2 Chron. 6:40; Isa. 43:25; Eph. 4:30; Heb. 4:13). That is, the Bible often describe God by using figures of speech and in human terms. These are used because they are easier to understand and invoke a response to who God is. They point us to what is true of God, but often in a devotional manner not achieved by technical theological language. One danger is to never take metaphors as literal descriptions of God, for this will result in a wrong understanding of God's nature.

If everything needs a cause, then so does God? The principle of causality used in the cosmological type arguments does not say everything needs a cause. It only states that every effect needs a cause. Both the Universe as a whole and its parts, every finite changing thing is an effect. Therefore, only finite changing things need causes. God is not an effect. Therefore God does not need a cause. He is the uncaused cause of all effects.

If God created all things then he must have created himself? God is not a thing, in the sense that he is finite or needs a cause. Self–causation is a contradiction. One cannot cause or create themselves; they would have to exist before they existed to cause themselves. God is uncaused or not caused. He does not need a cause or a creator since he has no beginning or end.

If God is the moral Lawgiver, then he decided what is right and wrong or the law is beyond him? These are not the only two options. It is possible, since God is all–good and loving, that the moral law is God's nature. Hence, it is not that God arbitrarily selected what would be good and bad or that the moral law is imposed on God from outside himself. Instead, it is His very nature and hence flows from Him.

Can God make a rock so large he cannot move it? This is actually a category mistake. It is like asking if there is anything greater than an infinite or can God make a square circle? You cannot ask the all–powerful being (i.e., God) if he is capable of having more power. Since God is all–powerful, he can do anything that is possible. There are some things God cannot do such as ceasing to exist (since He is a necessary being). God is not able to do what is actually impossible (i.e., make square circles). But he can create a anything that is possible, including a rock, as large as he wants and do anything with it that he wants to do. There is no way to be more powerful than that.

God must be good and evil, since he has no limits? God is unlimited in the sense that He is perfect and eternal. Evil is a lack or limitation in things. It is the absence of good where it should be. Evil is not something in and of itself. Since God has no lack or limitation in his attributes, such as goodness, He cannot also be evil.[11]

If God is a necessary being, why can't the universe be? Our observation of real things reveals that they exist, but they need not exist since they could cease to exist. They must therefore be dependent upon something that necessarily exists. By saying that God is a necessary being it does not mean that He must *do* everything out of necessity. It only means that he must exist in a certain way, and He cannot change what He is necessarily. He does not have to create anything. He may freely choose to do so, but nothing in God or outside makes Him create.

If God is eternal, when did he create the world? This is

---

11. See Norman L. Geisler, *If God, Why Evil?* (Minneapolis: Bethany House, 2011).

another category mistake. One cannot ask a time related question (i.e., when did . . .) to that which has no time or is eternal. Time is a measurement of change (befores and afters), and there was no change before creation. God did not create *in* time, He is the creator *of* time.

If God knows and controls everything then all is determined and there is no free will. God knowing everything humans *will* do with there freedom does not imply that God must determine *what* they do with their freedom. God created the capacity of free choice; but humans are responsible for their exercise of free choice. God can determine things in accordance with human free choice, but does not coherence or force free choice (since that is a contradiction).[12]

Arguments for God's existence, while not without critics, are sound and valid; hence they are demonstrative. While objections exist, they are not without answers and the theologian is on good philosophical ground to approach theology with this understanding firmly in place.

Questions to Answer
1. What is the best argument for the existence of God and why?
3. What implications are there for theology regarding arguments for God's existence?

Terms and Concepts to know:
Natural Theology
Agnosticism
Immanuel Kant
Kalām
Augustine of Hippo
Thomas Aquinas (Fifth Way)
Anselm
C. S. Lewis
William Paley
Cosmological
Teleological

---

12. Norman L. Geisler, *Chosen But Free*, 3rd ed. (Minneapolis: Bethany House, 2010)

Axiological
Ontological
Fallacy of Composition
Specified Complexity
Irreducible Complexity

Select Readings
Geisler, Norman L. *Philosophy of Religion,* Parts 2 & 4.
Lewis, C. S. *Mere Christianity*, Book 1.

5 Does the Christian God Exist?

Objectives
1. Explain how an argument for God's existence demonstrates that the Christian God exists.
2. Explain the nature of the Christian God.
3. Answer various objections to an argument for the Christian God.

An Argument for the Existence of the Christian God

What follows is a vertical cosmological argument that Theism, i.e., the belief that God exists, is true and that this God must be the God of the Christian Scriptures.[1] As such, the existence of the Christian God is established on rational grounds, apart from Scripture, and hence becomes the basis for all theological expression as well as the means to show that our theological understanding is correct. First we briefly state the argument and then discuss each premise in detail.[2]

---

1. This is a not an argument for the Trinity which is true of God, but is only known from and based on the authority of Scripture. See Geisler, *Systematic Theology*, Vol. 2, chapter 12.
2. Summarized from Geisler, *Christian Apologetics*, 265.

1. Something undeniably exists.
2. Nothing cannot cause something.
3. Something necessarily and eternally and exits.
4. I am not eternal and necessary.
5. Whatever is not eternal and necessary needs a cause.
6. Therefore there is an eternal and necessary cause of my existence.
7. This eternal and necessary cause must be all–powerful, all–knowing, all–perfect (or good) and personal.
8. This eternal and necessary cause is identical to the Being described as God in the Christian Scriptures.

1. Something undeniably exists. For example "I exist." It is impossible for me to deny my own existence. I would have to exist to deny my own existence. This argument is therefore reducible to a self–evident and undeniable first principle.

2. Nothing cannot cause something. It is impossible for something to come from nothing. Only nothing can come from nothing. Since there is something (i.e., I exist) it must have come from something.

3. Something necessarily and eternally exists. If nothing cannot produce something and something exists, then something must exist necessarily. This something that is necessary must be eternal. If it is necessary it cannot not exist. If it cannot not exist then it must have always existed or be eternal. Imagine if all the things you know about ceased to exist. What would be left? If you say "nothing would exists," then there is nothing to account for the things that exist. However, if you answer, "something would exist," then that something must have always existed and cannot not exist (be eternal and necessary).

Hence, an ontological description of a necessary being is possible at this point. If such a being exists it must be pure actuality with no potentiality (if it had potentiality then it would be possible for it not to exist), changeless (because it has no potentiality), nontemporal, non spatial (space and time involve change), eternal (cannot have potentiality to come to be), one (no way to differ from another in its being if no potentiality), simple (no principle of differentiation in it, so it must be undivided), infinite (only potentiality has limitations, pure actuality is being) and uncaused (caused passes from potentiality to actuality, but it has no potentiality hence it is uncaused).

4. I am not eternal and necessary. Not only can I not cause my own existence, I can also cease to exist. My non–existence is possible. I change in time, space (know from experience) and knowledge (the contrary is self–stultification). I am not alone because I use language to communicate with others. I cannot deny it without using it to speak to others. Although I exist, I have the potentiality not to exist. I am contingent as well as limited. If I can cease to exist then I am not necessary. I am contingent. What is left if all contingent things cease to exist? It cannot be nothing because something exists and nothing cannot produce something. It must be something that is necessary so that it can account for the something that is contingent and undeniably exists.

5. Whatever is not eternal and necessary needs a cause. By cause it is meant the actualization of a potential (i.e., what causes the transition from potentiality to actuality). Note that this kind of causation is simultaneous or causation *per se*. That which is potential existence is either self–caused, caused by another, or uncaused. Self causation is impossible. It cannot be uncaused because possibility cannot be the ground of actuality. Nothing cannot cause something. Therefore, it must be caused by another. Perhaps it can be seen more clearly by application to oneself. Because I am not eternal and necessary I need a cause. I know that I am not eternal and necessary because I can cease to exist. What can cease to exist cannot be eternal and necessary. I cannot cause myself. A self caused being is impossible. Because I am a may–be (possible) that is and not a must–be (actual necessity). I cannot be uncaused (potential actualizing itself). Therefore, I must have a cause outside myself. That is, something that causes me to be when I need not be nor continue to be.

6. Therefore, there is an eternal necessary cause of my existence. There cannot be an infinite regress of causes for my existence (i.e., one contingent being causing another contingent being *ad infinitum*). This is because there would be at least one cause that is both causing its own existence and the existence of another. But a self–caused being is impossible. Another way to see this is to point out that a contingent series either has a cause outside itself or within itself. If it comes from beyond then the series is dependent on a cause. If the cause is within the series then there is self–causality. Adding an infinite series does not provide an adequate ground of existing. Adding effects does not provide a cause (e.g., if a chain with five links needs a peg than an infinite chain needs an even stronger peg). Therefore, there must be an eternal and necessary uncaused first Cause for a contingent being or series of beings in existence.

7. This eternal and necessary cause must be all–powerful, all–knowing, all–perfect (or good) and personal. Since there is no potentiality or finitude in the infinite cause it cannot be like its effects in their potentiality. It can only be like its effects in their actuality. Therefore any finitude or limitation cannot be attributed to the uncaused cause. By power it is meant what effects a change in another (e.g., to cause to be or not be). Since the uncaused cause is infinite in its being it has no limit in its causal power. It has all power to do anything possible. An infinite cause must be all–knowing. This is so because caused knowing beings exist. This is undeniable. To deny that I am a knowing being, I must use my knowledge. The uncaused cause must contain all knowledge because it is eternal and the cause of intelligent contingent beings. By perfection or goodness it is meant that which is desired for its own sake. This is undeniable. The person denying goods is enjoying the good of being able to express this denial. The cause of good (in the becoming of good acts) must be (–ing) Good for He cannot give what it does not intrinsically have to give. Since the cause of all–goodness is infinite it must be infinitely good. I cannot deny the existence of personal beings. Such a denial involves the expression of personality and relies on the existence of other persons for communication. Since personal caused beings exist, the cause of personhood cannot be less than personal. Thus, the uncaused cause must be personal.

8. This eternal and necessary cause is identical to the Being described as God in the Christian Scriptures. The God described in the Bible is eternal (Col. 1:16; Heb. 1:2), changeless (Mal. 3:6; Heb. 6:18), infinite (1 Kings 8:27; Isa. 66:1), all–powerful (Heb. 1:3); Matt. 19:26), and all–loving (John 3:16; 1 John 4:16). There can only be one eternal being. If there were two then one would have something the other did not have. The being that lacks what the other one has would not be eternal and there would be only one eternal being. If both are the same then there would be no way to tell them apart and there would be only one eternal being. Therefore, the Being described in the forgoing argument is identical to the God described in the Bible. Hence, such a God as described in the Bible exists.

Some Objections Considered

Arguments do not demonstrate the existence of God. This mistaken notion usually arises as the result of confusion between two kinds of demonstration: propter quid with quia. *Propter quid* demonstrates the "whatness" of something. For example, proving that Morris is a cat involves an argument that matches all the characteristics of felineness (catness) with Morris to then conclude he is a cat, i.e., what it is. This is appropriate for reasoning with things found in the natural created world, but not for metaphysical being or God. For the existence of God, we must argue demonstration *quia*. That is, we examine effects and reason they must have a cause, i.e., that something is, even though we cannot match that cause with something else we know in the created world. This is still demonstrated knowledge, even though we do not know directly (only through its effects) the cause. This is the kind of demonstration made with respect to arguments for the existence of God.

Existential statements are not logically necessary. The basis of this cosmological argument is an existential statement such as "I exist." The objection to this is self-defeating. Consider the statement "No existential statements are necessary." Either this is a statement about existence or it is not. If it is a statement about existence then it is self-defeating. It claims to make a statement about reality. Yet, it denies the very reality that the statement itself must rely upon to be true. If it is not a statement about reality then it tells nothing about what kind of statements can be said about reality. The only way to deny existential statements is to make one in the act of denial. Thus, such statements are self-defeating.

The statement "I exist" does not have to be logically necessary. Non existence is not logically inconceivable. The statement is simply undeniable, because I do exist. Such a statement could not be made if I did not exist. The basis for this statement is ontological not logical. It is the fact that it contains an undeniable truth, not that its opposite is logically impossible.

Existential statements are *a priori* or apply to the mind only. It is important to distinguish this starting point from some other cosmological type arguments. For example, René Descartes (1596–1650) started with "I think, therefore I am." Descartes' starting point makes a claim about the existence of his knowing mind (i.e., self is prior to the world). It makes a claim about knowing that I am a knowing being, instead of making a claim about knowing reality outside one's own mind. Our statement (Something exists.), however, makes a claim about the undeniable reality of existing things. As one Thomistic philosopher clarifies,

> The Cartesian method arrives at the claim that the self is prior to the world, that our certainty of our own existence is greater than our certainty that the world exists. Indeed, we arrive at certainty of the existence of God *and then* derive from features of God the reliability of knowledge for the world. . . . [In contrast the classical view understands that] Everyone knows for sure things about the world; things whose existence cannot be coherently doubted. The things of the world are what we first know, and we become aware of ourselves insofar as we know the world. . . . Philosophy is not the study in which we for the first time come to know things for sure. Philosophy presupposes that we are already in possession of truth about the world and ourselves.[3]

To help clarify, our metaphysical principle of being or reality rejects or avoids (i.e., circumvents) the trap of purely transcendental (i.e., analytic) understanding of propositions and knowledge that always begins with thought and then tries to argue to God. This cosmological argument begins with being (or existence) itself

---

3. Ralph McInerny, *A First Glance at St. Thomas Aquinas* (Notre Dame: University of Notre Dame Press, 1990), 32, 34. This is the core distinction between the modern and classical (or Cartesian and Moderate Realist) method. See Etienne Gilson, *Thomistic Realism and The Critique of Knowledge,* trans. Mark A. Wauck (San Francisco: Ignatius Press, 1986).

which is undeniable and argues to the existence of God.[4]

This cosmological argument depends on the invalid ontological argument. This is not true of the above stated argument. This is because it begins with an existential premise (1) and proceeds, not on ontological ground, to a rationally undeniable principle (premise 2). This argument concludes with an unlimited cause of finite existence, as opposed to a being that logically cannot not be (premise 3). The argument is nowhere dependent on statements or claims that originate in the mind alone (i.e., *a priori*). Hence, it is not based on the invalid ontological argument. An ontological definition is assumed in completing the argument (premise 7), however, it is at no time a basis for the argument.

Since all things that undeniable exist are finite, only a finite cause needs to be inferred. This objection fails because it depends upon an infinite regress (see below) which is impossible. The first Cause cannot be finite or limited. For everything that is limited must have something limiting it. There must be something beyond it that is its cause of existence. This cause must be the Unlimited limiter of all other things. If it is unlimited then it must have no limits or be eternal and thus necessary (see premise 3 above).

An infinite series of finite effects is possible. There must be a ground for the existence of a series of causes. If there is not then they do not exist because nothing has a real ground for its existence. But if the series is grounded then there must be a first Cause. There cannot be a cause causing its own existence. A self caused being is impossible.

Further, an actual infinite series is impossible. Theoretical or mathematical infinities are possible but they are not real. It is impossible to have an actual infinite number of books. Another book can always be added. No matter how thin the pages there cannot be an infinite number. A series of real finite beings must be limited. If it were real it could be added to and thus it would not be infinite. Therefore, there must be a real cause or ground for finite

---

4. For a critique of Kant's division of propositions into analytic (necessary truths) and synthetic (contingent truths) see Henry B. Veatch, "St. Thomas and the Question, 'How Are Synthetic Judgements A Priori Possible?'" *The Modern Schoolman* 42 (March 1965): 239–263.

beings.

The importance of this rational argument in theology is not only that God exists and that this God is the God of the Bible (since, some doing theology deny this), but also, and perhaps more importantly, is that God's nature must be a certain way (e.g., unchanging). Therefore, we must approach theology and scriptural study with this understanding of God firmly in place as we seek to do theology.

Questions to Answer
1. Does this argument actually demonstrate the existence of God? why or why not?
2. What is the difference between Descartes' and Aquinas' starting point in their argument for God's existence?
3. How can an argument for God's existence show that the God of the Bible must exist?
4. From this argument what can you conclude about the nature of God?

Terms and Concepts to know:
Thomas Aquinas
René Descartes
Act
Potency
Necessary existence
Immutable
Eternal
Simple
Uncaused
Self–caused
Caused
Demonstration *propter quid*
Demonstration *quia*

Select Readings
Geisler, Norman L. *Christian Apologetics*, chap. 15.
Gilson, Etienne. *Methodical Realism*.

6 Are Miracles Real?

Objectives
1. Define a miracle.
2. Describe the confirming nature of miracles.
3. Identify the fallacies in arguments against miracles.

What Are Miracles?

Christianity is rooted in the miraculous. If miracles are impossible, then the Bible is not true and Christianity is false. The Apostle Paul admitted this when he said, "If Christ has not been raised, then our preaching is vain, your faith also is vain. Moreover we are even found to be false witnesses of God, because we testified against God that He raised Christ, whom He did not raise, if in fact the dead are not raised. For if the dead are not raised, not even Christ has been raised; and if Christ has not been raised, your faith is worthless; you are still in your sins" (1 Cor. 15:14–17).

What is a miracle? Both theists and atheists have generally agreed on a definition of a miracle. David Hume (1711–1776) said "Nothing is esteemed a miracle, if it ever happened in the common course of nature. It is no miracle that a man, seemingly in good health, should die all of a sudden; because such a kind of death, though more unusual than any other, has yet been frequently observed to happen. But it is a miracle, that a dead man should come to life; because that has never been observed in any age or country."[1] Contemporary philosopher Antony Flew likewise asserted: "A miracle is something which would never have happened had nature, as it were, been left to its own devices."[2]

Hence, a miracle is an event that is beyond the power of nature to produce; an event that can only be explained by positing supernatural (God's) power. As such, it should not be confused with what may happen that is an unexplained natural event such as an anomaly or something providential such as surviving a car accident that should have killed a person. It is not an illusion or trick preformed by a magician. It is not even something supernormal which might be done by the power of a created spiritual being (i.e., angel). These may be classified as unusual events but they are not miracles.[3]

Three philosophers have raised objections to miracles. Benedict Spinoza's *Tractatus Theologica–Politicus* questioned the possibility of miracles. David Hume in his *An inquiry Concerning Human Understanding* questioned the credibility of miracles. Anthony Flew in an article titled "Miracles" in the *The Encyclopedia of Philosophy* questioned the rationality of miracles. Since Theism holds that God has intervened in the course of history, it is necessary to examine and answer these arguments.

Are Miracles Possible?

Benedict Spinoza's (1632–1677) reasoned as follows concerning the possibility of miracles:[4]

---

1. David Hume, *An Enquiry Concerning Human Understanding,* 3d ed., rev. (Oxford: Clarendon, 1975), 1: 33, 115.

2. *Encyclopedia of Philosophy*, 5:346.

3. See Norman L. Geisler, *Signs and Wonders* (Wheaton: Tyndale House, 1988).

4. Adapted from Norman L. Geisler, *Miracles and the Modern Mind.* Grand Rapids: Baker, 1992, 15. See Beneditc de Spinoza, *A Theologico–Political Treatise and A Political Treatise,* Trans. R. H. M. Elwes. (New York Dover, 1951), chap. 6.

1. Miracles violate natural laws.
2. Natural laws are unchangeable.
3. Unchangeable natural laws cannot be violated.
4. Therefore, miracles are impossible.

The theist, however, will point out that Spinoza has presented an argument that begs the question of miracles (*petitio principii*). He has assumed naturalism (that there is no God) in his definition of natural laws. However, if natural laws do not describe unchangeable patterns, then the question of miracles is still open. As C. S. Lewis asserted, if you admit God, then miracles are always possible.[5] If this is true then natural laws only describe general patterns. Natural laws are descriptive of natural events in our world. They are not prescriptive in the sense that they determine what must happen. Hence, what is not unchangeable can have exceptions. Miracles are exceptions to, not violations of, the general pattern of nature. What Spinoza failed to do was to provide some sound argument for his naturalistic presupposition.

Are Miracles Credible?

David Hume presents arguments against the credibility of miracles. His first argument is against the principle and practice of miracles. His next argument is against miracles in religion. His first argument goes as follows:[6]

1. A miracle is a rare occurrence (by definition).
2. Natural law is a description of regular occurrence.
3. Evidence for the regular is always greater than for the rare.
4. A wise man bases his belief on the greater evidence.
5. Therefore, a wise man should never believe in miracles.

There are two interpretations of this argument. The first one is a hard interpretation that believes Hume is saying miracles are actually impossible. The second is a soft interpretation that believes Hume is saying one should just never believe in miracles because the evidence will never be sufficient (at least compared to the evidence for natural occurrences). It is important to understand that

---
5. C. S. Lewis, *Miracles*, (New York: MacMillian, 1960).
6. Adapted from Geisler, *Miracles*, 27. See Hume, *Enquiry*. chap. X.

in this second interpretation Hume is not understood as arguing for the impossibility of miracles but only the incredibility of accepting miracles.

If the hard interpretation of Hume is correct, then the theist's response is virtually the same as our response to Spinoza. He begs the question in favor of naturalism by defining miracles as impossible. Our answer is to present the case for theism and define miracles as exceptions rather than violations.

If the soft interpretation prevails, then the theist's response of miracles is not ruled out entirely. They are simply held to be incredible based on the evidence. The wise person does not claim they cannot occur, only that they should never be believed. However, at least one or two errors prevail if we take this approach. First, Hume assumes the uniform experience for all humanity throughout time. How does he know that all experience is uniform? Does he have access to all experience past and future to make such a claim? If not then he begs the question. Second, it could be that Hume is selecting the experiences of some persons who have not encountered miracles. If this is the case then he is committing the error of special pleading. C. S. Lewis responded to this very understanding of Hume by saying: "Now of course we must agree with Hume that if there is absolutely 'uniform experience' against miracles, if in other words they have never happened, why then they never have. Unfortunately we know the experience against them to be uniform only if we know that all the reports of them are false. And we can know all the reports to be false only if we know already that miracles have never occurred. In fact we are arguing in a circle."[7]

Hume's argument is further weakened by pointing out that he is adding evidence versus examining evidence. For example, if Hume adds up all the incidence where people have died and not been raised and uses it to overwhelm any possible evidence that anyone has raised from the dead then he commits the fallacy of truth by majority vote (*consensus gentium*). He is equating the quantity of evidence with probability or quality of evidence. Such a view would eliminate belief in any unusual or unique event from the past. If this is true, then one should never believe in three dice

---

7. Lewis, *Miracles*, 102.

showing three sixes since the chance is 216 to one. Or one should never believe that a perfect bridge hand is possible since the odds are 1,635,013,559,600 to 1. This view also confuses the *basis* of knowledge with the *object* of knowledge. For example, the basis of belief in a supernatural event can be the regular observations (that people die and stay dead), while the possibility of an exception or miracle can be the object of our knowledge even though it is a singular occurrence. In short, this argument of Hume's proves too much: If it is true then we should not believe a miracle even if it happens!

In Hume's next argument he reasons that all religions use miracles to support their claims. This concerns the actuality of miracles, that is have any occurred, and if so what is the confirming value of such events if they have occurred. Hume reasons since all, or most, major religions claim miracles as confirming acts of God. How can miracles confirm any one religion as true? Consider a specific example. If Christianity claims miracles and Islam claims miracles, then miracles cannot be used to confirm either. It would seem they cancel each other out as a confirming act.

We can briefly point out that this objection wrongly assumes that the evidence for miracles provided in one religious system is the same in all of them. But if they are not of the same nature, then a canceling disproof for miracles in religious systems can actually be used to confirm a religion's unique miraculous claims. For example, one might argue that the miracles of Christianity, because they are rooted in history with credible eyewitness accounts, when compared to other religions becomes plain to see that the evidences are not the same kind. Hence, it may be possible (as apologists do) to argue that only Christianity has unique miracles confirmed by sufficient testimony and evidence. Therefore, only Christianity is divinely confirmed by miracles. If the testimony concerning miracles can be established on historical grounds, then the verification of Christian miracles serves as canceling test of other religions that claims miracles. God, because of his nature, would not verify two religions opposed in their essential teachings. Therefore, only one religion can have confirming miracles from God.

Are Miracles Irrational?

Antony Flew offers us the final argument we will consider. He says miracles are just irrational. He reasons:[8]

1. Miracles are particular and unrepeatable.
2. Natural events are general and repeatable.
3. The evidence for the general and repeatable is always greater than that for the particular and unrepeatable.
4. Therefore, the evidence against miracles is always greater than for them.

Admittedly the argument of Flew is not much different then Hume's. Hence, the theist's answer is not very different then the response given to Hume. Naturalism is presupposed in the definitions given. However, it is worth pointing out that if miracles are to be rejected because of naturalistic unrepeatablity, then much of science that believes in a singular origin of the universe and of life should also be thrown out. This view also creates a naturalistic unfalsifiablity. No matter what actually occurs, regardless of the evidence to the contrary, we are obligated to believe it was not a miracle. This is hardly a scientific approach that is open minded. Furthermore, it is worth pointing out that evidence for the repeatable is not always greater. If this is true then almost all unusual events of historical and scientific significance should be abandoned since they only happened once and are unrepeatable. Some might try to strengthen Flew's argument by countering that miracles are not credible in a scientific age. But this, again, assumes that there is no God and that everything calls for a natural explanation. That every event needs a natural explanation is not something discovered by science, it is philosophical. Just because our age is dominated by a scientific mind set does not mean miracles cannot occur or not be proven to have occurred. The possibility of miracles must be decided on the philosophical question regarding the existence of God. The question of the actuality of miracles must be decided on the question of historicity (i.e., is there evidence for a miracle).

So what can miracles accomplish? Let us first point out one thing they cannot accomplish. They cannot be used to demonstrate the existence of God. That is the task of natural theology (see chap-

---

8. Adapted from Geisler, *Miracles*, 34. See *Encyclopedia of Philosophy*, 5:346

ter 4). For example, if it is proved that Jesus rose from the dead. It will not necessarily convince those holding to a different world view that God raised him from the dead. An atheist simply can conclude that it is an anomaly that will someday be explained by natural causes. A pantheist may conclude Jesus was just a man that demonstrated advanced manifestation of deity that we can all strive to emulate because we have the same potential. Neither view is forced to accept belief in the theistic God, given the historical proof of the resurrection of Jesus. The existence of God is logically and necessarily prior to the acceptance of a miracle as proof for anything.

However, having said that, miracles can be used to help adjudicate between religious claims. Given the truth of God's existence, miracles with corroborating historical proof can be used to confirm a message from God. The Bible contains about 250 miracles and 60 are in the Gospels (Ex. 4:1–9; Matt. 12:38–39; Luke 7:20–22; John 3:1–2, Acts 2:22; Heb. 2:3–4; 2 Cor. 12:12). For a miracle to serve as a sign from God it is necessary that it be attached to a truth claim from God (Matt. 12:38–39), be multiple (Acts 1:3; 28:9) immediate (Matt. 8:3; 8:13) and contain predictive elements (Matt. 12:40; John 13:19). Only these criteria separate miracles from what could be construed as just unusual events or from claims in other religions opposed to Christianity.

Some theologians reject claims to the miraculous in the biblical text. However, given the apologetic truth of Christianity, any theological approach to the Scriptures, which denies the supernatural involvement, must be rejected. This does not mean everything a naturalistic theologian would say about the Bible is wrong, but it does cause us to question any theory or view that relies on a purely natural explanation to the origin or content of the scriptural text, especially when it claims a supernatural event (i.e., miracle).

Questions to Answer
1. Describe an event that would be a miracle?
2. How does one's world view affect the theological value of miracles?
3. Describe the major flaws of David Hume's argument against miracles?

Terms and Concepts to know:
Miracle
Natural Law
Benedict Spinoza
David Hume
C. S. Lewis
Anthony Flew
petitio principii (begging the question)
consensus gentium (truth by majority vote)

Select Readings
Geisler, Norman L. *Miracles and the Modern Mind.*
Geisler, Norman L. *Signs and Wonders.*
Hume, David. *Enquiries Concerning Human Understanding* chapter X.

7 What is Man that He Can Know?

Objectives
1. Describe the problem of universals.
2. Explain the implications of the hylomorphic view of reality.
3. Explain why humans must be a soul/body unity.

How Do We Know?

This question, although epistemological, is related to metaphysics. Notice that we are not asking the question, Do we know or can we know?, but *How* do we know? It seems quite clear that we know, to deny this affirms the self–defeating nature of skepticism. In answering this, we must avoid the problems evident in critical realism and idealism. Both views always begin with thought, and try to argue to the existence of an external world. If thought unsuccessful the result is idealism, if thought successful then realism. But the existence of a real world is already evident to us and therefore does not need to be proved. As Frederick Wilhelmsen shows us: *"Man knows there are things because he senses them."*[1] From

---
1. Frederick D. Wilhelmsen, *Man's Knowledge of Reality* (Englewood Cliffs: Prentice–Hall, 1956), 31, emphasis his.

the time we are infants we know all kinds of things even without much thought involved. But to answer the question how do we come to know will take some thought. As we will see, our answer to the question will also give us a glimpse into the very nature of reality and humanity.

It will help to observe reality again and consider a well known problem in philosophy: Universals. These are objective categories or concepts that contain every item of a class (sometimes called genus or species). For example, consider our example of a real tree. What makes us classify it as a tree? Any one quality of a tree considered in isolation such as its colors (brown and green), its height (20 feet), its trunk, branches, and leaves does not constitute the classification of a tree, but put them together and that is what everyone says it is. This is because all the objects that meet the qualities of a tree are universally recognized as this particular concept or category which also excludes all other classes. However, we experience only particular instances of this tree or that tree. We never find the "ideal" or universal class of a tree in reality apart from its expression in a particular tree. Yet, at the same time, we create from the particular its universal class and call it what it is. Even if all particular trees went out of existence, we could still exemplify the universal concept. Hence, universals such as treeness do not depend upon particulars. Are these universals real? How we answer this question will directly affect our answer to the question of how we know reality.

There are four answers to the question of universals: 1) Absolute Realism says universals exist in themselves (Plato); 2) Conceptualism says universal exist as categories in the mind with no relation to things outside the mind (Kant); and 3) Nominalism denies any universals outside or inside the mind (William of Ockham 1288–1348). Any position that denies universals cannot answer how everyone calls something the same thing without depending upon universals in their explanation and the objectivity of concepts to do so. Everyone calling a tree "green" and having the same concept of greenness is unexplainable apart from universals being real, participating in particulars and being objective concepts, as opposed to subjective, in our minds. Furthermore, all of these explanations create a separation or dichotomy between the knower and reality.

However, only 4) Moderate Realism[2] reveals a path to how we know by explaining that universals are grounded in reality by virtue of the forms or essense of things and can come really to exist in the intellect. Physical objects exist independently and they do not depend on our mental processes to exist. In other words, there is a real external world that can be known. We must recognize that the problem is more than a logical one. It is primarily metaphysical. Universals must apply to every particular or it is not a universal and they (universals) can have a form of existence in the mind of a knower. Hence, only Moderate Realism is able to account for how we can really know reality.

As you may remember from chapter 2, all finite beings are composites of actuality (existence) and potentiality (to change). Existence or *esse* is the act by which an essence (what something is) has being. Again, these are principles in a being and not things in themselves. An essence is further composed of substance and accidents. For example, a human being is a substance.[3] But the fact that he or she is a certain color, height, weight, etc. is accidental to the substance. Accidents do not exist apart from substances. You cannot, for example, find the color white apart from a substance. Accidents can change; such as a human who tans in the Sun undergoes a color change. Substances cannot undergo this kind of change. A human essence cannot become a cat essence or vice versa. The substance is that which remains the same even though accidental qualities may change through time. We know substances through our five senses of seeing, smelling, hearing, tasting, and touching.

A substance can further be explained by the relationship of form and matter. This is how we come to know substances in reality. The form of something is related to its actuality; form is what something is (i.e., an essence). For example, a cat has the form of

---

2. "Moderate" in realism is to designate the position that holds universals really do come to exist in the intellect, but their existence stops there (moderate).

3. The term "substance," in Aquinas, seems to be limited to knowable individuals naturally occurring in the world. It should not be confused with subsistence. Something can have subsistence with no subject. "Humanity" for example is a subsistent reality but it does not have to have a substance.

catness, and a dog has the form of dogness. Matter is related to the individual potentiality (to change). It is that which individuates an essence to be this cat (or that cat). Matter, as used here, should not be equated with physical matter, and form should not be equated with the shape of something. Instead, these are principles of finite substances in reality. The form of a substance is immaterial. The matter of a substance is what individuates the essence to be a particular thing (that gives it extension in space) which is limited to its individualized form. We can say a dog is not a cat because of their different form or essence. We can say this cat is not that cat because of their different matter. The way in which we know something is by its form, which is united to matter. We know a substance (individual form/matter) via our five senses which data is put together and processed by our internal senses. Since the form of a substance is immaterial, it is able to enter our mind and we are able to know the substance as it is in itself. Our intellect is able to abstract the universal from the individualized form.

It is very important to understand that the form, which enters the mind, is not a different substance or copy of the substance that is outside the mind. The same form that is united with matter outside the mind unites with the mind of the knower. In a sense the knower and the thing known become one and is therefore not something subject to physical or scientific examination. This view avoids Cartesian/Kantian representationalism and/or idealist epistemology that shifts the knowing of things to the consciousness of the mind rather than the thing in itself and a purely naturalistic view that denies any reality to the immaterial. What we have explained here is known as the hylomorphic[4] view of reality in Moderate Realism. Contemporary philosophers representing this approach include Étienne Gilson (1884–1978) and Joseph Owens (1908–2005).

Things do not exist because they have matter, but because they have an act of existence. Likewise, individual man is a compound of accidents that differentiate him from other men. All of his particular accidents make him an existing individual. Yet, his form of essence, his humanness, makes him what he is, i.e., a man. Thus,

---

4. All natural things change (i.e., accidentally and substantial change such as that which terminates their being) including human beings contain two principles of reality: matter (Gk. *hyle*) and form (Gk. *morphe*).

his essence must differ from his individuality.

Exploring this question, gives us the opportunity to establish on philosophical grounds that the intellect of man must be immaterial. Mortimer Adler (1902–2001), states the case:

> Whatever exists physically exists as an individual, and whatever has individuality exists materially. No one has ever experienced or produced anything that has physical or corporeal existence and also is a universal in character rather than individual. . . . Our concepts are universal in their signification of objects that are kinds or classes of things rather than individuals that are particular instances of these classes or kinds. Since they have universality, they cannot exist physically or be embodied in matter. But concepts do exist in our minds. Hence that power must be an immaterial power, not one embodied in a material organism such as the brain.[5]

This observation, supported by common experience, seems to be a good argument to establish that man must be a composite or unity of intellect (or soul) and matter (or body).

What is Man?

Since we have established the necessity of a material and immaterial aspect to man, it only remains to establish the nature of this immaterial/material or soul/body relationship. While many answers have been offered to this question,[6] we can cross off any theory that embraces Materialism, which claims that only the body exists, and that there is no soul (Thomas Hobbes 1588–1679) or Idealism, which claims that only the soul exists and that there is no body (George Berkeley 1685–1753). It seems that the predominate theory today is Dualism (or Dichotomy) in which soul and body are separate and parallel entities that never intersect. This theory was first attributed to Plato but is classically expressed by Descartes:

---

5. Mortimer J. Adler, *Intellect: Mind over Matter* (New York: Macmillan, 1990), 50.
6. See Richard Taylor, *Metaphysics*, 4th ed. (Englewood Cliffs: Prentice Hall, 1992), 16ff.

> Thus, simply by knowing that I exist and seeing at the same time that absolutely nothing else belongs to my nature or essence except that I am a thinking thing, I can infer correctly that my essence consists solely in the fact that I am a thinking thing. It is true that I may have (or, to anticipate, that I certainly have) a body that is very closely joined to me. But nevertheless, on the one hand I have a clear and distinct idea of myself, in so far as I am simply a thinking, non–extended thing; and on the other hand I have a distinct idea of body, in so far as this is simply an extended, non–thinking thing.[7]

The Cartesian view, however, is philosophically rejected for at least two reasons. First, it assigns the higher cognitive processes to the soul only, since the human being is a soul residing in a body. That is the person is not identical with his body. This makes it impossible for the soul to interact with the body since the body is an extended substance which can only act upon and be acted upon by other extended substances. Hence a solution must be found which leads to the second problem. Some third medium or locus, another spirit or bodily organ, must be postulated in order to unite the soul to a body. However, distinct substances cannot be bound together unless something unites them. Hence, we must abandon any view that sees them as separate.

The metaphysical anthropology of Aristotle and Aquinas avoids these problems by expressing the soul/body unity which is in line with the hylomorphic understanding of reality. The soul is the substantial form of the human body. As one evangelical Thomist states, "The form is what distinguishes one species from another, it is the soul, the seat of the intellectual faculties, that we must look to for the form of man. The body is physical matter distinguished from other physical matter by the soul, and the whole complex is man. Man is not the soul by itself, let alone only the body, but the entire body–soul unit."[8] This view clearly avoids the Cartesian problems since the body/soul is a causal unit, and, at the same time, different functions can be attributed to each: such as

---

7. *Meditations on First Philosophy, Book VI* trans. John Cottingham et al. *Descartes Selected Philosophical Writings* (New York: Cambridge University Press, 1994), 114–115.

8. Winfried Corduan, *Handmaid to Theology: An Essay in Philosophical Prolegomena* (Grand Rapids: Baker, 1981), 50.

the fact that the body eats and the soul thinks. There are also some functions, such as emotions (e.g., grief) and pain, which affect both body and soul. Hence, it seems that there is some philosophical reasoning to support a theology that humans are a soul/body unity capable of knowing reality.

Humans *know* because they are a soul/body unity that experiences the world via sensory input in which the intellect is able to extract and classify *forms* that are the identical *forms* (not a representation) in sensible reality.

Questions to Answer
1. What is the hylomorphic view of reality?
2. How do we come to know sensible reality?
3 Give a philosophical argument for the immaterial (soul) nature of man.

Terms and Concepts to know:
Absolute Realism
Nominalism
Moderate Realism
Conceptualism
Universals
Essence
Substance
Accedent
Form/Matter
Hylomorphic
Étienne Gilson
Joseph Owens
Dualism/Cartesianism
Body–Soul Unity

Select Readings
Adler, Mortimer J. *Intellect: Mind over Matter*.
Wilhelmsen, Frederick D. *Man's Knowledge of Reality*.

SECTION THREE
Epistemology (TRUTH)

Epistemology studies the nature of knowledge, its presuppositions, foundations, its extent and validity. It addresses questions such as: What is knowledge? What does it mean to know? How do we know, and what is truth? To accomplish the goal of our study we will limit ourselves to these questions: What is truth? (chapter 8) Is there a correct theory of truth? (chapter 9) How do we reason? (chapter 10) Can we talk about God? (chapter 11) Is an objective Interpretation possible? (chapter 12) And finally, is history knowable? (chapter 13) If truth is relative, then what we claim is true about God and our theology is only relative and not necessarily true for everyone. If however, truth is absolute then theological truth is true for all people at all times in all places. If our language about God is not meaningful or it is not possible to arrive at an objective understanding then theological truth becomes unobtainable. If however these are possible, then theology can make truth claims and can express truth about God.

8 What is Truth?

Objectives
1. Define absolute and relative as they relate to truth.
2. Give a reason as to why there is no such thing as a relative truth.
3. Explain why relativism does not apply to truth in religions.

Truth: Relative or Absolute?[1]

Allan Bloom opened his book *The Closing of the American Mind* by making an alarming assertion: "There is one thing a professor can be absolutely certain of: Almost every student entering the university believes or says he believes that truth is relative."[2] Our society has been described by many as post–modern. Modernism at least considered the question of truth worth asking and perusing. But post–modernism does not even consider the question relevant. Truth for post–modernism, including theological truth, is completely relative. What is true for me may not be true for you. Is

---
1. This discussion follows that found in Norman L. Geisler, *Introduction Bible*, Vol. 1 *Systematic Theology* (Minneapolis, Bethany House, 2002), 118–120.
2. Allan Bloom, *The Closing of the American Mind* (New York: Simon and Schuster, 1988), 23.

there such a thing as absolute truth?

Let's first define what we mean by relative and absolute. Relativism needs to be understood in two senses. First, there is the sense of relative to space and time. Something was true then (in the past) but it is not true now (in the present) or something was true there, but it is not true here. Therefore it is relative with respect to time and space. Second, a relative truth can also be understood as something that is true for a person. It is true for me, but not for you. An absolutist approach affirms that if something is true it is absolutely true. Whatever is true at one time and in one place is true at all times and in all places. Likewise, whatever is true for one person is true for all persons.

It is important to clarify a truth claim. It is not just a phrase about which there is no question of truth such as "a clear day." Also it is not just opinion or something that we could not have knowledge about or a way to know if it is true or false. It must be a statement that affirms or denies something knowable. Such as, "It is a clear day today" or "Ronald Reagan is President of the United States." Is this statement true? Since Reagan was president only from 1980–1989, it is false. The relativist would say this is an example of why truth must be relative. Since Reagan is not now president; the statement would only be true if it was said during his presidency. Such a truth only applies to a certain time and place. However, the absolutist would say if this was said in 1985 it would be an absolutely true statement and if it was said today that "Ronald Reagan is president" it would be false unless it added "from 1980–1989," then it would also be absolutely true. In other words, it will always be true for all people, in all places, and for all times that "Ronald Reagan was president from 1980–1989." If it is true for all people, in all places, for all times it is absolute. There is nothing relative about that.

What about personal statements such as, "I feel cold." Is that not relative to me? Everyone certainly does not necessarily feel cold or my coldness. But notice that the claim is not about every one, it is about me. It is true for everyone, in all places, at all times that I feel cold. Hence, it is an absolute truth. If someone at the same time says "I feel warm" then it is an absolute truth that they feel warm regardless of what others may feel at the same time and place.

It is important to recognize what is being claimed to be true. Some one may have said in 1000 BC "I believe the Sun goes around the earth." If so, it will always be true for all people that some ancient human believed the Sun goes around the earth. It does not mean it was true in ancient times that the Sun goes around the earth, and it is false now (because we know the earth moves around the Sun). False beliefs, even though they are false, may be believed nonetheless. What is true is that they are believed, and this must be absolute.

What about comparisons such as height, is it not relative to call someone tall and another short? Again one must look at what is being claimed to be true. If John is taller than Bob, then it will always be true that John is taller than Bob (given that they have both stopped growing) for all people, in all times, and places. What we compare things to may change, but the truth claim (that someone is taller or shorter) will never change and is either right or wrong.

The truth of the matter is there is no such thing as a relative truth. If something is true, then it must be true for all people, in all times, and places. Hence, it is absolute. One does not have to have absolute evidence or proof for something to be an absolute truth. Levels of certainty exist within differing subjects. Some subjects, such as philosophy make deductive arguments from metaphysically undeniable statements about reality while others work inductively to establish probabilities such as science or history. We may know some truth claims with greater or lesser certainty than others, but this does not affect the absolute nature of truth itself. Also, as indicated above claiming to *believe* something is true, is not the same as a truth claim (i.e., that it is true). Many people believe false things. What is absolute about these is that they believe it, not that what they believe is necessarily true. Such belief must still be tested according to the nature of the subject to discover its truthfulness.

Refuting Relativism

Relativism as an overall system of understanding truth contains many unsolvable problems. First, if relativism is true then there could be contradictory truths within our world. This is not just a contradiction in truth claims, such as "I believe man is finite" and another claim that says, "I believe man is infinite." But actually the case that man is finite and infinite. Second, if relativism is true, then nothing could really be known to be true or actually be true. Historical questions such as "who won World War II?" or scientific questions such as "what is energy?"—may never be definitively answered or known. If relativism is true, we would have to admit that nothing could be unchangeably true. Third, it follows that if truth is relative, then we could never learn or be mistaken. Everything we learned in school may not be true in another part of our world or at another time. Making an error or getting a question wrong on an exam has no significance, since in another part of the world or in a different period of time those answers may be true.

Furthermore relativism is completely unlivable. Who can live in a world where saying "yes" is the same as saying "no?" Ten dollars could be the same as one million dollars. Communication as well as trust would be impossible. Finally, complete relativism is self defeating. It asserts that truth is relative, but such an assertion relies on the notion that there is an absolute truth namely the theory of relativism. Is the theory of relativism absolute or relative? If absolute, then it is not true that all truth is relative. If relative, then it is not necessarily true for everyone.

Some may respond that they believe only some areas are relative such as religion or theology. What one believes about God is true to them, but not necessarily true for others. But it is impossible to make such a line of demarcation. One can claim that they "believe god is finite" or "believe that God is infinite" but it cannot actually be the case that God is finite and infinite. Likewise, contradictory religions cannot both be true. Christianity and Islam cannot both be true, since they disagree on such fundamental beliefs as the nature of God (Ti–unity vs. absolute monotheism). Furthermore, one claims Jesus died and was raised from the dead, and the other denies this. Hence, religious truth is subject to the same inquiry as other truth claims, and therefore, cannot be relative.

Refuting Relativism in Religion

Some may suggest that even if relativism does not apply to everyday truths, it does nonetheless apply to religion or especially the notion of knowing transcendence. Religious relativism is the belief that each religion is true to the one holding the belief. Religious pluralism, on the other hand, is the belief that every religion is some how true. The later we have already addressed by refuting the notion that truth is not something that is personal or subjective, but is absolute and objective. The nature of truth is such that it cannot be different for everyday decisions vs. religious beliefs.

John Hick is perhaps the most prominent scholar promoting a view of religious pluralism. He believes that no religion can have the true understanding of God or in his terms "the Real" since all religions fundamentally disagree on who or what is transcendent. He believes a distinction should be made "between the noumenal Real, the Real *an sich*, and the Real as humanly perceived in different ways as a range of divine phenomena."[3] Hence, there is an unbridgeable gap that exists between all the world religions and exactly what is the Real. So his advice to adherence of any specific tradition is to stay in one's tradition realizing that it is one among several ways of approaching, understanding, and experiencing the ineffable Real.

The problem with this view is that Hick has appealed to the wrong discipline to settle the question. Hick appeals to the conflicting knowledge of the great world religions to discover that no one can advance a truth claim about the Real's nature which is superior to any other claim. However, as Aquinas would remind us, it is not to the teaching of the world religions that one must appeal, but to the use of natural reason which is common to all regardless of religious persuasion.[4] In the area of metaphysics (see section 2), this is achieved by offering a proof or argument that the Real exists and is capable of communicating objective truth with humans or that human language is adequately able to express objective forms of meaning (see chapter 12).

---

3. John Hick, *A Christian Theology of Religions* (Louisville: Westminster John Knox Press, 1995), 68.

4. Thomas Aquinas, *Summa Contra Gentiles* I,2.3.

Hick's dichotomy is further challengable by the observation that 'nothing but statements' imply more than knowledge. If Hick is going to claim that all religions of the world are unable to know the 'Real' in itself then he must have 'more knowledge' of the Real to know that none of the religions have true knowledge about it. But this of course is self-defeating according to Hick's own hypothesis. Namely, that no one (including Hick) can know the Real in itself. Such statements, however, imply that more is known about the Real in itself than to say that no one else knows. In short, he must know more about the Real than any one else in order to claim that no one else knows the Real in itself.

So, What is Truth?

When answering the question of what is truth, it is hard to improve upon Aristotle's: "To say of what is, that it is not, or of what is not, that it is, is false; while to say of what is, that it is, and of what is not, that it is not, is true."[5] Truth, in short, is that which corresponds to reality. To say it is anything else is to end up affirming a self-defeating proposition. If we claim "we do not know reality," we must ask how we know the reality of that very statement. If we say, "Our senses are unreliable" we must realize that we have depended upon our senses to make and communicate such an assertion.

Relativism is self-defeating in that it is unable to account for its own assertions without appealing to absolute truth. Furthermore, it is completely unlivable as a consistent system whether dealing with everyday issues or religion. Truth no matter what area it is in, must be absolute. As we demonstrate in the next chapter, the correspondence understanding of truth is the only adequate explanation of truth.

Questions to Answer

1. Draw a chart comparing the relative and absolute nature of truth.
2. Give a defense of the absolute nature of truth?

---

5. *The Complete Works of Aristotle*, ed. Jonathan Barnes, Vol. 1 metaphysics (Princeton: Princeton University Press, 1984), 4.7.1011b25–9.

3. What implications are there for theology regarding the absolute or relative nature of truth?

Terms and Concepts to know:
Relative
Absolute
Truth
Religious relativism
Religious pluralism
John Hick

Select Readings
Geisler, Norman L. "Religious Pluralism: A Christian Response"

Geisler, Norman L. *Systematic Theology*, Vol. 1, chap. 8.

9 Is there a Correct Theory of Truth?

Objectives
1. Explain the Correspondence Theory of Truth.
2. Critique each of the non–correspondence theories of truth.

Theories of Truth

When we speak of a theory of truth, it is an acknowledgement that there are different definitions for understanding the nature of truth. As such, this should not be confused with a test for truth. A theory of truth answers the question, "what is the nature of truth?" A test for truth, answers the question, "How do we know something is true?" Hence, a test is a defense of truth, while a theory explains the nature of truth. There are four basic theories of truth: 1) Coherence theory of truth, 2) Pragmatic theory of truth, 3) Internationalist theory of truth, 4) Correspondence theory of truth.

Coherence Theory of Truth

The coherence theory of truth states that something is true if and it coheres or is consistent with other truths of the system. Each affirmation about truth is related to other statements from which truth is derived. For example, imagine a primitive tribe or culture deep within the rain forest that had never seen frozen water. This theory suggested that because nothing in their system allows for an understanding of frozen water, for them it is not true. This system suggests that something is true only when it is able to be integrated with other truths into a coherent system that agrees. If the item is not integrated into the existing system, then it cannot be considered true. One consequence of this approach is that individual truth claims (or statements) are really only partially true or partially false. They are dependent upon the system as a whole for their integration. Only the whole system is considered completely true. Many philosophers have supported this understanding of truth including: Spinoza (1632–1677), G. W. Leibniz (1646–1716), Georg Hegel (1770–1831), and F. H. Bradley (1846–1924).

There is at least one positive feature of this system. It validly assumes that truth must cohere. It is necessary for truth not to contradict itself. However, just because two things agree with one another does not make them true. There must be some other grounds on which to incorporate truth. In short, the coherence theory of truth is necessary, but it is not sufficient. The theory of coherence may completely contain truths that have no application to empirical knowledge. It may completely contain truths dependent upon mathematical assertions which apply only to the mind. This may interest the mathematician, but truth that does not make a claim on reality, is not going to do anyone any good. A system that does not need anything to apply to reality is not going to offer any correspondence to reality. Furthermore, the coherence view is unable to adjudicate between two different coherent systems that agree internally. It is conceivable at least to even have two opposing coherent systems that are contradictory. With no way to discover by coherence which one is true, we are left with an inadequate theory of truth.

Pragmatic Theory of Truth

The pragmatic theory of truth states that something is true, if and only if, it has practical consequence that are beneficial to an individual or group (society). If something does not benefit an individual or group, then it should not be considered true. For example, as applied to religious beliefs, such would only be considered true if it benefits the believing individual or group. If it helps the person survive and properly function in society or feel competent to be a contributing member of society, then the religious belief is considered true in the practical sense. If, on the other hand, the religious belief is harmful to individuals or society, then beliefs must be considered untrue in the practical sense. The theory rests on the notion that what works best, is always true. As long as it is working, then it is considered acceptable and true. Once this criterion is lost, then what ever it is must be discarded and considered false. Philosophers that have supported this approach to truth include Charles Pierce (1839–1914), William James (1842–1910), and John Dewey (1859–1952).

There are several difficulties with this view. First, the notion that something is true, if and only, if it "works" clearly introduces an ambiguous and somewhat subjective notion. What works for one person or group may not work for another. Something may also have worked in the past, and that same thing does not work in the present. How is one to decide what is true in these cases? Second, consider two people: one believes it is a beautiful sunny day outside (when it is not) and the other believes it is a beautiful sunny day outside (when it is). Both individuals experience the beneficial attitude change that results from a sunny day. However, the theory is unable to explain any beneficial difference between it actually being sunny out, and believing it is sunny out. According to the pragmatic theory, just believing it is sunny out, truth wise, is the same as it actually being sunny out because both individual benefited from the belief. Third, some things may actually work that are false. Telling a lie or pretending to be someone else may help you achieve a beneficial goal such as getting promoted or earning more money. Such may even benefit society as a whole if you're going to be president. But many things may be morally wrong or just false that are a benefit for the individual or society. Finally, this theory is subject to its own criterion. How does one know, what if any, are the beneficial consequences of the pragmatic theory itself? If we are unable to know the consequences of this theory, as to whether it works or not; why accept it? It can be rejected based on its own criterion.

Intentionalist Theory of Truth

The intentionalist theory of truth is a subset of the pragmatic view which has significant implications for theology and particularly biblical inerrancy. It states that an author's statement is true, if and only if, it accomplishes what it was intended to accomplish. If it did not accomplish what was intended then it is false. Admittedly this view is most often brought forward by biblical scholars who want to avoid the conclusion that the Bible's inspiration involves inerrancy. Such individuals see no need for a God inspired Book to be true in scientific, historical, or other earthly matters as long as its spiritual message (what was intended) is accomplished. In short, if the Bible communicates what the author(s) intended it to, then it is true. A prophet or apostle could have been wrong in giving the exact location of a city, date, name of a leader, or even have depicted inaccurate historical events, but if what he intended to communicate about God and heaven is accomplished, then it is true. Two theologians supporting this view of truth are G. C. Berkouwer (1904–1996) and Jack B. Rogers.

There are some serious problems with the intentionalist view of truth. First, something may achieve an intended result that is factually inaccurate. I could easily write out false directions as to how to get to a city with all the best intentions of getting you there. You may even end up at the city I intended for you to reach. But if the directions are false, then according to this view they are true. Furthermore, the reverse is also possible; I could intend to deceive you but inadvertently give you correct directions. According to this view, the directions I gave you are actually false because my intentions were to give you miss–directions. With the possibility of such nonsensical situations arise as a result of this view; it is hard to take it seriously as a view of truth, much less as support for a theory of inspiration. This view is basically saying persons (as far as their intentions go) are true or false, not statements. It certainly is enough to make one wonder if we know what the intentions were of those that developed the intentionalist theory of truth.

Correspondence Theory of Truth

The correspondence theory of truth says that something is true, if and only if, it corresponds to reality. As Aristotle succinctly stated, "To say of what is, that it is not, or of what is not, that it is, is false; while to say of what is, that it is, and of what is not, that it is not, is true." All the other views we have examined are non–correspondent views. Mortimer Adler reminds us that,

> The correspondence theory asserts (1) that there is a reality independent of the mind, and (2) that truth (or, what is the same thing, knowledge) exists in the mind when the mind agrees with, conforms or corresponds to, that independent reality. When what I assert agrees with the way things really are, my assertions are true; otherwise they are false. . . . The principle of noncontradiction is both an ontological principle (the principle that contradictories cannot coexist in reality) as well as a logical rule (the rule that thinking cannot be correct if it is self–contradictory).[1]

Aristotle and Aquinas both approached the topic of truth with this understanding. Some contemporary Philosophers explaining this view of truth include G. E. Moore (1873–1958), and Alfred Tarski (1902–1983).

There is much support for the correspondence theory of truth. First, lies are impossible without a correspondence view of truth. If one's statements need not correspond to the facts in order to be true, then any factually incorrect statement could be true. And if this is the case, then lies become impossible because any statement is compatible with any given state of affairs. Second, without correspondence there could be no such thing as truth or falsity. In order to know something is true as opposed to something that is false, there must be a real difference between things and the statements about the things. But this real difference between thought and things is precisely what is entailed in a correspondence view

---

1. Mortimer J. Adler, *Intellect: Mind over Matter* (New York: Macmillan, 1990), 98–99.

of truth. Third, factual communication would break down without a correspondence view of truth. Factual communication depends on informative statements. But informative statements must be factually true (that is, they must correspond to the facts) in order to inform one correctly. Further, since all communication seems to depend ultimately on something being literally or factually true, then it would follow that all communication depends in the final analysis on a correspondence view of truth. Finally, even the non–correspondent theories depend on the correspondence view of truth. Since all of the non–correspondence theories claim their theory is a true account of truth corresponding to our world. So without correspondence one cannot even make theoretical claims to explain the nature of truth.

Does the Bible Support a Correspondence View of Truth?

If the correspondence view of truth is philosophically correct and the Bible is true, one should not be surprised to find assertions in Scripture that depend on the correspondence view of truth. Many scriptural passages and commands assume a correspondence view of truth for their assertions to be true. For example: The ninth commandment depends on a correspondence view of truth. "You shall not give false testimony against your neighbor" (Ex. 20:16). Moses commanded that false prophets be tested on the grounds that "if what a prophet proclaims . . . does not take place or come true, that is a message the Lord has not spoken" (Deut. 18:22). Something was considered a "falsehood" if it did not correspond to God's law (truth) (Ps. 119:163). Jesus' statement in John 5:33 entails a correspondence view of truth: "You have sent to John and he has testified to the truth." Paul clearly implied a correspondence view of truth when he wrote, "Each of you must put off falsehood and speak truthfully to his neighbor" (Eph. 4:25).

Some have objected to the correspondence view by asserting that some verses appear to contradict the correspondence view. For example Jesus said, "I am the way, the truth, and the life, . . ." (John 14:6). Some assume this means truth is personal (since Jesus was a person) not propositional. But upon closer examination of the theory, it becomes clear that this cannot be the case. Consider the claim that "all truth is personal, not propositional." Let me ask you, is that claim a proposition or a person? Of course, and if it is a proposition then by its own criterion it must be false. Furthermore, Jesus does, have correspondence. He must correspond to his words, deeds, and the will of the Father. These are all things to which he must correspond to be true.

Another objection concerns truth and God. Some claim that if truth is that which corresponds to reality and God is true, then God must correspond to something beyond. We have already answered this by arguing for the existence of God (see chapter 5). There we reasoned that something must be ultimate to account for the existence of anything else. Since God is ultimate, the only thing to which the ultimate can correspond is Himself. All of God's thoughts are true to Himself. Hence, God's correspondence begins and ends in Himself.

All non–correspondence views of truth secretly depend upon the correspondence view of truth. Hence, the correspondence view of truth is the only adequate explanation of truth. All of our experience, including Scripture, testifies to this. Hence, this must be the understanding of truth we apply to all aspects of our theological work.

Questions to Answer
1. Explain how all non–correspondence theories of truth ultimately rely on the correspondence theory of truth.
3. Give a defense of the Correspondence theory of truth?
2. What implications are there for theology regarding different theories of truth?

Terms and Concepts to know:
Test for Truth
Theory of Truth
Coherence
Pragmatism
Intentinalist
Correspondence
John Dewy
William James
G. C. Berkouwer

Jack B. Rogers
Aristotle
G. E. Moore
Alfred Tarski

Select Readings
Geisler, Norman L. *Systematic Theology*, Vol. 1, chap. 7.
Geisler, Norman L. "The Concept of Truth in the Inerrancy Debate"

10 How Do We Reason?

Objectives
1. Clarify the relationship between God and logic.
2. Identify the premises, conclusion, and terms of a deductive argument.
3. Distinguish between deductive and inductive reasoning.

Laws of Thought

The term "logic" is used to describe the rules that are used to discover correct and incorrect reasoning. One text states, "Logic is a way to think so that we can come to correct conclusions by understanding implications and the mistakes people often make in thinking."[1] All reasoning is built on fundamental laws of thought that are inescapable. Logic is necessary to all thought. Since theology is reasoning (*logos*) about God (*theos*), it is necessary here too.

There are three fundamental laws of all thought:

---

1. Norman L. Geisler and Ronald M. Brooks, *Come Let us Reason* (Grand Rapids: Baker Books, 1990), 13.

1. Law of non–contradiction (A is not non A).
2. Law of identity (A is A).
3. Law of excluded middle (either A or non–A).

If the law of non–contradiction does not apply, then it is impossible to distinguish something from being God and not being God. One could never affirm that something is not God or something is God. If the law of identity does not hold, then it is impossible to affirm God is God or that God is identical to Himself. If the law of excluded middle did not apply, we could not affirm anything about God or not about God. Any thought about God cannot escape these principles.

Some have questioned why these laws ought to be accepted. Some schools of Eastern thought, for example, say that they do not apply to what is Ultimate. The Ultimate is beyond all reasoning and categories of thought. However, it is important to realize that these laws are self–evident. Because of that, there is no direct defense to be offered for them. Once they are understood or realized, they defend themselves. It is enough to show that any attempt to deny them is self–destroying. If I say, "There is no law of non–contradiction" I have not only assumed the law, I have affirmed its existence in the very statement. If I say, "God is beyond the laws of logic." I have assumed the laws in that very statement since its opposite is being denied.

Questions about God and Logic

There are some questions and objections concerning the relationship between God and logic that should be answered. Some have objected that we are making God subject to human logic.

Is logic prior to God? To answer this we must separate the question in two spheres of inquiry: metaphysics and epistemology. Since God's existence and being are identical He is the basis of all logic (ontologically speaking). However, logic is the basis for all human knowledge about God (epistemologically speaking). In other words, logic is prior to God in the order of knowing, but not in the order of being.

Is God subject to our logic? This question assumes it is our logic. Humans did not invent logic; it is discoverable by humans.

Since God is the author of rational thought, he is not subject to logic. Rather, linguistically speaking it is our statements about God that are subject to logic. When we apply logic to God (or, statements about Him) He is not being tested by a standard outside Himself since logic flows from His rational nature.

Can God violate or break logic? Some believe since he can do the impossible He should be able to break the laws of logic. However, while God can do what is humanly impossible He cannot do what is actually impossible (Heb. 6:18; 2 Tim. 2:13). To ask if God can violate logic is to ask if he can do something against his nature. God cannot break logic anymore than he can change His nature. The laws of logic are not similar laws of nature that are descriptive. Natural laws describe the way things normally occur. Logic, on the other hand, is prescriptive in that it is the way we should always think. In this sense logical laws are similar to ethical laws.

Is there more than one logic? Some say there is an eastern and western logic, why should we choose one over the other? Actually, since all logic depends on the same undeniable law of non–contradiction there can only be one logic. Since there is no other basis or other rules for logic, there cannot be more than one.

Do biblical doctrines violate logic? Some believe that biblical doctrines such as the Trinity, Incarnation, and Predestination involve contradictions. There is an important distinction, however, to make between an actually contradiction (i.e., paradox) and a mystery. There is no actual contradiction concerning these doctrines as presented in Scripture because there can be no contradiction in God's nature. If there is what appears to be a contradiction, then it is the result of fallible human reasoning, not a perfect divine Being. But there can be mysteries in Scripture that go beyond finite human reason and understanding.

Kinds of Reasoning

The three laws of logic make it possible to draw rational inferences that form a valid (or sound) conclusion. There are two kinds of reasoning in which this can be done. 1. Deductive also called *a priori* (ah pree–oh–ree), which means prior to looking, starts with a cause and reasons to an effect. 2. Inductive also called *a posteriori* (ah paw–ster–ee–oh–ree), which means after looking, starts with the effect and reasons to a cause.

Deductive logical arguments are constructed with syllogisms. A syllogism contains a major premise, minor premise, and a conclusion. For example:

    1) All A is inside B.
    2) All B is inside C.
    3) Therefore, All A is inside C.

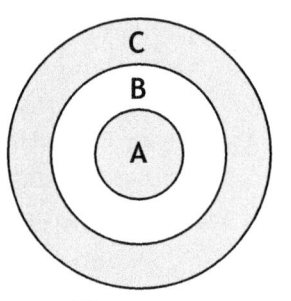

Figure 10.1
Deductive Syllogism

Each sentence is given a designation as follows.

    1) Major premise: All A is inside B.
    2) Minor premise: All B is inside C.
    3) Conclusion: Therefore, All A is inside C.

There are also terms associated with each sentence. For example,

    1) All saved persons *(middle term)* are believers *(major term)*.
    2) All born again persons *(minor term)* are saved persons *(middle term)*.
    3) Therefore, all born again persons *(minor term)* are believers *(major term)*.

Deductive reasoning involves arriving at a necessary conclusion. It is important to distinguish between the truth of an argument and the validity of the argument. Truth is concerned with examining the parts to see if they correspond to reality. This is called material logic. The validity is concerned with the formal structure of the argument. This is called formal logic.

Inductive reasoning, as opposed to deductive, does not arrive at a true/false conclusion. Instead, it is based on probability of varying degrees. Another way to think of the different kinds of reasoning is to consider deductive reasoning to be from general statements to a particular conclusion. For example,

1) All human beings are rational beings. (General)
2) Mary is a human being.
3) Therefore, Mary is a rational being. (Particular)

Induction, on the other hand, reasons from particulars to a general conclusion. For example,

1) Human beings such as Matthew, Mark, Luke, and John, and others have one head.
2) Therefore, all human beings have one head.

Induction usually does not result in an absolute conclusion (since all humans have not been observed). Instead, induction is a generalization or extrapolation based on known evidence. However, a perfect induction is possible, if every case is known to be observed. Usually when the induction is limited to a certain set of criteria, it can be perfect. For example if I say every coin in my pocket is a quarter. It is possible for this to be verified and it would be a perfect induction. This is important to theology, because the Bible is a fixed area of criterion. There are only 66 books which are limited in content. Hence, a perfect inductive argument is possible if every verse or instance of something is examined.

There are two basic kinds of probability to make inductive arguments. The first is *a priori* probability (prior to and independent of the facts). This is usually mathematical in nature dealing with the odds. For example, what is the likelihood of getting three sixes on a roll of three dice before they are tossed? The answer is 1 in 216. Theologically we would ask what are the odds that nine Messianic prophesies could be fulfilled by chance? The answer would depend on the number of Messianic prophesies calculated from Scripture. The second kind of inductive reasoning is *a posteriori* probability (arising after examining the facts). This is empirical or scientific probability. This involves the arriving at a probable conclusion based on observations of the natural world. Many scientific theories and laws have developed as a result of this kind of reasoning. This type of reasoning is also important for systematic theology, because some theories may agree or disagree with theological conclusion. For example, the big bang theory seems to agree with Genesis 1:1. However, the theory of evolution (life arising by chance) clearly disagrees with Genesis 1 and 2.

It is also important to realize that, according to rules of induc-

Informal fallacies: Ambiguity and Relevance

Fallacies of Ambiguity

Simple Ambiguity: Occurs when a phrase or word is used with two or more meanings.
Amphibole: Occurs when the words are clear in meaning but the grammar is not clear.
Accent: Occurs when the tone of voice changes the meaning.
Significance: Occurs when conditions or circumstances change the meaning of words.

Fallacies of Relevance

1. Approaches that include attack.
   Argument ad Baculum: one tries to persuade by force.
   Argumentum ad Hominem (abusive): one tries to persuade by assassinating ones character (i.e., showing that the person is bad, not the argument).
   Argumentum Hominem (circumstantial): one tries to persuade by showing a bad circumstance surrounding a person.

2. Approaches that include inappropriate authorities.
   Argumentum ad Ignorantiam: assumes it is true unless shown to be false.
   Argumentum ad Misericordiam: appeals to pity or emotion to prove their point.
   Argumentum ad Populum: appeals to opinion polls or popularity to prove their point.
   Consensus Gentium: appeals to what the majority opinion is to prove a point.
   Argumentum ad Vercundiam: appeals to authorities to prove their point.
   Argumentum ad Annis: appeals to time as an authority, the age of it determines its validity.
   Argumentum ad Futuris: appeals to the future to support its position.

3. Fallacies of stacking the Deck
   Petitio Principii: is circular reasoning; the premise contains the conclusion.
   Straw man: creates a false picture of an opposing argument and then refutes it.
   Special Pleading: appeals to only some evidence to support a view and leaves the rest of it out.

4. Fallacies of Diversion try to win by changing the subject.
   Ignoratio Elenchi: focuses on a related but irrelevant conclusion to prove a point.
   Red Herring: changes the subject to divert attention away from the relevant issue.

5. Fallacies of Generalization try to fit everything into a few categories.
   Dicto Simpliciter: applies a general rule to a particular case that is different then the general case.
   Hasty Generalization: uses an atypical case to support one point, concludes too much from too little.
   Cliché: might suffer from oversimplification or appeal to a popular maxim.

6. Reductive Fallacies considers only one aspect of a complex issue.
   Nothing–Buttery: argues that something is only one (nothing but) aspect of it.
   Genetic Fallacy: argues that something is wrong because of the origin of the idea.
   Complex Question: asking one question that really contains two questions to show that an implied answer proves their point.
   Category Mistake: wrongly mixes one category with another to prove a point.
   Faulty Analogy: arguing by analogy that is not relevant to the issue.
   Argument of the beard: blurs the distinction between things by appealing to the differences only in degree of things.

Many other types of fallacies exist: faulty dilemma, hypothesis contrary to fact, prestige jargon fallacy, slippery slope fallacy, fallacy of composition, and fallacy of division.

Figure 10.2 Informal Fallacies

tive and deductive logic, there are varying degrees of certainty. Absolute certainty is really only achievable for deductive reasoning; as long as the argument is valid and the premises corresponds to reality. Practical certainty is possible for induction, however even here if every case is examined a perfect induction is possible. Another area of certainty important to theology is moral certainty. This is possible based on moral, psychological and/or spiritual factors such as in the case of assuring salvation (Rom. 8:16).

Logical Fallacies

There are two kinds of fallacies related to argumentation. Formal fallacies cover errors in the way an argument is put together. This usually concerns the placement or use of some of the terms in an argument. Informal fallacies are errors in clarity or soundness of the reasoning process. The two major types of informal fallacies are 1) fallacies of ambiguity: in which case the meaning is not clear; 2) fallacies of relevance: in which case the argument does not address the right issue. Figure 10.2 contains a list of some of the most common informal fallacies.

Correct reasoning is indispensable to theology. Our understanding of God as well as scriptural doctrines must be expressed in ways that are sound and valid which do not involve formal and informal fallacies

Questions to Answer

1. Identify each sentence and term of the following argument by filling in the blanks:

   1) _____: All saved persons _____ are believers _____

   2) _____: All Christians _____ are saved persons _____

   3) _____: Therefore, all Christians _____ are believers _____

2. Explain the difference between deductive and inductive reasoning.

Terms and Concepts to know:
   Logic
   Argument
   Logical necessity

Premises
Conclusion
Inductive Arguments
Deductive Arguments
Major term
Minor term
Validity
Form (of argument)
Soundness
Tautologies
A priori
A posteriori
Equivocation
Formal Fallacies
Informal Fallacies

Select Readings

Kreeft, Peter. *Socratic Logic*.

Geisler, Norman L. *Baker Encyclopedia of Apologetics*, "Logic" & "Inductive Method"

11 Can We Talk About God?

Objectives
1. Explain realism's view of language against conventionalism and essentialism.
2. Defend the use of language as it relates to descriptions about God.

Language and Meaning

It is important to first address the fundamental question concerning language and meaning. This subject is known as semantics. Of course it is self-defeating to say "language contains no meaning." Since the very sentence assumes that language does contain meaning. However, the question of how meaning is related to language is still important. Is it objective or relative? And how does it actually relate to language? There are three views of how language and meaning are related. The first is **conventionalism**. This states that all forms of meaning related to language are relative. Hence, the essence of language is temporal. Meaning, in other words, is relative and culturally dependent. Our society has developed a language and a corresponding meaning that is culturally relative. For example, we know what snow is because we have experienced it. But a primitive culture located in a region that has never experienced snow, has no idea what it is. Even describing it to them in their own language would not help. Ludwig Wittgenstein (1889–1951) held this view of language.

The second view is **essentialism**. This says that the essence of language are objective and eternal forms of meaning correspond to everything that is said. Beyond the world there is an eternal reality to which our language corresponds perfectly. For example, what we call "snow," has a perfect eternal form to which it corresponds in a one–to–one relationship. Plato held this view of language.

The third view is **realism**. This says there are objective forms of meaning that we can express in our language. Our language is adequate to account for the different forms. For example, you may experience snow on multiple occasions and describe it differently each time. However, there are some things you would describe about snow each time you experienced it that are the same. For example, it was white; it was cold, etc. These things that are always common to snow are what makes snow what it is. Regardless of ones language, the same things are said about it. Hence, objectivity is grounded in the thing that is experienced. This is a one–to–many relationship since the one thing (e.g., snow) can be described in many ways. Thomas Aquinas held this view of language.

There is an important clarification to make before proceeding. There is something about language that is conventional. Words are fundamentally conventional symbols. This must be the case since some words can serve more than one use. For example, the term "bark" can be used to describe the noise a dog makes or used to describe the outer lining of a tree. So the word itself is not essential it is conventional. This stands true for many other words such as board, ball, instrument, plane, etc. However, there are words that resist this kind of multiple usage. Some words seem be the same in all languages. For example, "buzz," "splash," and "boom" are words that mean the same in every language because they are tied to the very sound it tries to imitate. These are called onomatopoeia. But other than these, words have been selected based on conventional use. Another important distinction is that meaning itself is not conventional. In fact, words, except for instances of onomatopoeia, do not have meaning. They only have meaning in so far as they form a unit of meaning usually in a sentence. This must be true since it is self–defeating to assert the sentence, "No sentence has any meaning."

Evaluation of Language and Meaning

There are a number of difficulties with our first option concerning meaning and language: Conventionalism. The first is that it is clearly self–falsifying. For example the statement "all linguistic meaning is conventional (relative)" is itself not a conventional statement. It is relying on an absolute understanding of language to communicate its truth. Second, if conventionalism were correct, then there would be no universal truths or universal statements that would translate into all languages. For example, "all husbands are married" translates as a universal truth in all languages. Third, if conventionalism were true we would not know any truth prior to knowing the conventions of that truth in that language. But we know, for example that 2 + 2 = 4 before we know the conventions of a language. Fourth, the laws of logic clearly present a challenge to conventionalism. Such laws as non–contradiction are not based in human words or symbols. They are true apart from all linguistic conventions. We do not choose our logic, we simply discover it. Fifth, if conventionalism were correct, no meaning at all would be possible. For if all meaning is derived from a cultural experience that can change over time, then there is no absolute ground for meaning. An infinite regress of meaning results since there is no absolute unchanging basis. Sixth, related to this is that conventionalism can only have a circular justification. At best it relies on a test for truth that is coherence. But an internal criterion cannot adjudicate meaning from different world views. For example if we read in the Bible "in Him we live and move and have our being." A pantheist may interpret that differently than a theist. The pantheist will say the world is God and the theist will say God is the transcendent creator of the world. Conventionalism has no way to discover which interpretation is correct since its view of language is relative to the world view. Finally, a truly descriptive knowledge of God is not possible in a conventionalist view of language. At best it can tell us what God is in our experience, but not what he is really in Himself.

Essentialism as an option for meaning and language does not fair much better. The fact, which we have already pointed out, that words have no real meaning (since they can be used to convey different meaning in different contexts) makes the idea that every word has an eternal absolute form to which it must correspond impossible. If words had eternal essences, then meaning (and truth) would change with every language. Furthermore, it really turns language into a god(s). It makes finite ideas or expression in language into an infinite idea (which only God can have).

Can Language Apply to God?

There are only three options when considering the nature of religious language or God–talk. Those holding that religious language is **equivocal** believe words apply to God in a totally different way than they apply to us. It is claimed that an infinite God transcends the ability to be expressed in finite language. A **univocal** understanding sees words as applying to God in exactly the same way as they apply to humans. The **analogical** view contends that language is applied to God in a similar way.

Equivocal. Plotinus (205–270 BC) and Moses Maimonides (1135 –1240) expressed different versions of the equivocal view. Plotinus believed that no positive descriptions can be made about God (or Unity). The term "One" used by Plotinus is only a term negating that God is a plurality. Likewise, only negative statements such as "One has no knowledge" or "One has no power" can be used to describe God. Plotinus argued that the One is Ultimate and there are no more ultimate terms by which the One can be described. The One is nothing but itself. No terms can really describe it. Positive names such as Good, beauty or Being can only describe His emanations. Even these are only extrinsic attributions. It is not that God is called Good because He possesses goodness but because he causes goodness.

Moses Maimonides agreed that God–talk is mostly negative, but he added that it does possess a positive aspect. God's essence, he believed, is unknown and cannot be described. Yet, language can positively describe God's activities. One can know what God does and speaks, but His essence or goodness cannot be known.

A serious problem with this view is that all negations imply prior affirmations. No one can say that God is not something unless he has some prior understanding of God. Another problem is that such a position results in self defeating claims and contradictions. Advocates of this view uses many words to describe God whom they say is not describable. The assertion, "words cannot be used to describe God" is self defeating since it describes something about God. Furthermore, everything that is affirmed about God is eventually denied about Him. Such contradictions clearly lead to total skepticism.

Univocal. Duns Scotus (1265? – 1308) expressed a univocal concept of God–talk. This view believes that religious language must have a univocal concept or the only result is agnosticism. Terms such as "good" must have the same meaning or concept when applied to man and God. If not, then you cannot know anything about God.

This view of religious language has a number of problems. First, this view cannot account for the infinite nature of God and the finite nature of humans. It is impossible to apply our finite concepts to an infinite God so that their applications are univocal, i.e., the same; since humans are not infinite. Thomas Aquinas likewise, argued that there is no way that God who is the creator can be equal to his creations (or effects). God is simple and His creatures are complex. Therefore, language cannot be applied to both in entirely the same way. Second, no created being can have the same being or existence as God. God is infinite and eternal. Therefore, no characteristic can describe both God and creatures in exactly the same way. Finally, to speak about two entities they must share common characteristics. They can differ in some way, but they also must be similar. However, God does not share His essence with any other being (there can only be one infinite and eternal being). Therefore, nothing can be said that applies univocally to God and creatures. This view, in the end, either makes man into God or God into man.

Analogical. Both equivocal and univocal views of language about God are unacceptable. Thomas Aquinas presents the only alternative which is analogical. This view sees language about God as a truthful analogy to the way it is understood on an infinite level by God. God is pure Act and humans are act and potency (limitations). Terms can be analogical because both God and man have actuality in common. But they cannot be applied univocally because only humans have potency. In other words, the terms can be *defined*[1] the same but they cannot be *applied* in the same way. Even before a term can be applied to God it must have all aspects of finitude negated. A term such as "goodness" must have all forms and contexts of finitude removed. Only the infinite and perfection of goodness can be applied to God. In short, God has goodness infinitely, and man has it finitely.

Concept – univocal	John has being	God is Being
Application – analogy	man – limited way	God – unlimited way

Figure 11.1 Analogical God–Talk

Some have objected to this view on the basis that many effects do not resemble their cause. Why should God resemble His cause, i.e., man in anyway? Another objection involves the seeming arbitrary selection of things in this world to be applied to God. Why are goodness and truth selected and not evil and falsehood?

The basis for such similarity, however, is found in the intrinsic relationship between humans and God. This is opposed to an extrinsic relationship or causation. For example, when you place an egg in boiling water the hardness that develops in the boiled egg has an extrinsic relationship to the water (which is not hard). There is no hardness in water whether it is hot or cold. But it does have an intrinsic relationship to the heat that is in the egg since it is able to make the egg hot when the water is heated. In a similar manner, there can be an intrinsic relationship between God and man. Only things that are intrinsic to man and God, such as being (i.e., existence) can be applied to both. Furthermore, only essential causes, not accidental causes, can be applied to God. Having a tall human body or short human body is an accidental quality. But the fact that one is an existing human being is an essential quality attributable to God's causation. Evil or falsehood cannot be applied to God because it is an extrinsic cause. Evil is a lack or privation in

---

1. This is not to suggest that meaning as understood and applied to God cannot exceed our understanding, but that there must be some level of univocity.

essentially good things. Goodness and truth, on the other hand, are essentially intrinsic causes and can apply to both humans and God.

In summary, if we follow the equivocal (what we say about God is entirely different) view of language applied to God it leads to skepticism. If we follow the univocal (what we say about God is entirely the same) it leads to a dogmatic assertion that man or his language is the same as God. Only analogy offers an acceptable way that says we can know and say some true things about God. For example, "being" that which is or has existence means the same (univocal concept) for God and finite man, but it is applied by analogy or only similarly to an infinite God who *is* being and finite man who *has* being. The views and positions in this chapter can be summarized in the following chart (Figure 11.2).[2]

	Essentialism	**Conventionalism**	**Realism**
Theory of Truth	Correspondence (one-to-one)	Coherence (or pragmatic)	Correspondence (many to one)
Truth	Absolute (unchanging)	Relative (changing)	Absolute truth in relative terms (words)
Essence of Language	Eternal form	Temporal forms	Eternal expressed in temporal
God–Talk	Univocal	Equivocal	Analogical
Representative	Plato	Wittgenstein	Aquinas

Figure 11.2 Meaning & Language

Questions to Answer

1. Define equivocal, univocal, and analogous as it relates to descriptions about God.
2. How can language be descriptive of God?
3. How does analogy, as it relates to God–talk, make theology acceptable.
4. Draw and fill in by memory the charts in Figures 11.1 & 2.

Terms and Concepts to know:

Semantics
Conventionalism

---

2. Adapted from Norman L. Geisler, *Prolegomena*, Class Notes (Southern Evangelical Seminary, 1996).

Essentialism
Realism
Universal
Equivocal
Univocal
Analogical
Via negative
Intrinsic causation
Extrinsic causation
Accidental causes
Essential causes

Select Readings

Geisler, Norman L. *Systematic Theology*, Vol. 1, chap. 9
Geisler, Norman L. *Philosophy of Religion*, Part 3.

12 Is an Objective Interpretation Possible?

Objectives
1. Describe how one comes to know a text.
2. Defend objectivity in interpretation.

Presuppositions and Objectivity

Since much of theology concerns the examination and interpretation of written texts whether it is Scripture, or other historical writings, it is imperative to establish the possibility of objectively interpreting such writings. Otherwise, theological truth from these writings is not obtainable.

A subjective theory of interpretation was influentially held by Martin Heidegger (1889–1976), Rudolf Bultmann (1884–1976), and Jacque Derrida (1930–2004). Such an approach argues that in interpretation there is one thing universally acknowledged: When a reader comes to any given text they come with presuppositions or preunderstanding. These include the point of view, background, assumptions and overall world view of the interpreter. Likewise, it is agreed that an interpreter cannot completely separate himself or herself from their presuppositions. Hence, there is no such thing as an interpreter completely devoid of one's presuppositions. This has lead many to conclude that an objective interpretation is not possible. With so many different interpretations there seems to be no way to tell whose interpretation is finally correct.

Such a view is clearly grounded in a conventionalist view of meaning. This, however, has been shown to be false (see chapter 8). Yet, a subjective theory of interpretation is claiming, "There is no objective interpretation." If the statement is true, then it must apply to every interpretation including any interpretation of this very statement. But this would seem to entail that there is some objective or universal truth or principle of interpretation since it is applicable to all interpretations. In other words, should we interpret the statement, "There is no objective interpretation" subjectively or objectively? If objectively then it is false. If subjectively then it is not applicable to all interpretations and the door is open to the possibility of objectivity. As Thomas A. Howe explains,

> The fact of the matter is, objectivity is not only possible, but it is also unavoidable. Even the critics of objectivity think that you, as a reader, can objectively understand their objections to objectivity. The reason it is important to establish that objectivity is possible is that without it there could be no communication. There would be no way to know whether we had correctly understood what was said or whether our preunderstanding had entirely distorted it.[1]

There is no doubt that some of our preunderstanding or perspective is unique to us, based on our experience, culture, world view, etc. It is interesting that everyone acknowledges that a reader comes to a text with presuppositions and is not able to separate completely from these. Even one who says, "I will come to the text objectively," is bringing this presupposition to the text. But it is in these acknowledgements that we are able to see an example of objectivity. Regardless of background, presuppositions, or world view everyone has acknowledged the presence of a readers presuppositions. Hence, there is something common and objective about this very claim that demonstrates the possibility of objectivity. Ob-

---

1. Thomas A. Howe, "Practical Hermeneutics: How to Interpret Your Bible Correctly (Part Two)," *Christian Research Journal* 25 (2003).

jectivity is possible because there are principles of communication that are universal. Such first principles we have already identified include the absolute nature of truth itself and the law of non–contradictions (see chapter 10). Because of this it is possible to use logic, first principles and reasoning to reduce conflicting interpretations and test them according to principles of interpretation in order to adjudicate between opposing interpretations. This is not to say all disagreement can be resolved and every mystery disclosed. But such work is worthwhile given there exists an absolute Mind that knows everything. Hence there is an absolute perspective by which objectivity may be approached and known. This was demonstrated in our argument for the existence of God (see chapter 5). Since there is an eternal absolute understanding, by analogy finite minds may have an adequate objective interpretation.

What is the Cause of a Text?

Before answering the question on how do we know a text, it is helpful to identify the causes of a text. Remember Aristotle's four causes from chapter 2. Since a text is created by humans these causes are best understood through artifacts. For example, when a carpenter makes a chair, there are several causes involved in the total process that results in the finished product (i.e., the chair). The same stands true for the process of producing a written text. To better identify these causes we first look at what goes into making an artifact such as a chair. The *efficient cause* that *by* which the chair is made is the carpenter himself. Second, is the structure of the chair which is called the *formal cause* that *of* which the chair is made. Third, is the *material cause* that *out* of which the chair is made (e.g., wood). Aquinas added two more causes which include the *exemplar cause* that *after* which the chair is made (e.g., drawing plans) and the *instrumental cause* that *through* which the chair comes to be (e.g., tools). Lastly, there is the *final cause* that is the reason *for* which the chair comes to be (e.g., to sit on).

Given these causes, regardless if we can identify them, any effect can have these causes involved. Since a written text is an effect, the causes of it can all be identified. The writer is the efficient cause of the meaning of a text. The writing is the formal cause of its meaning. The words are the material cause of its meaning. The

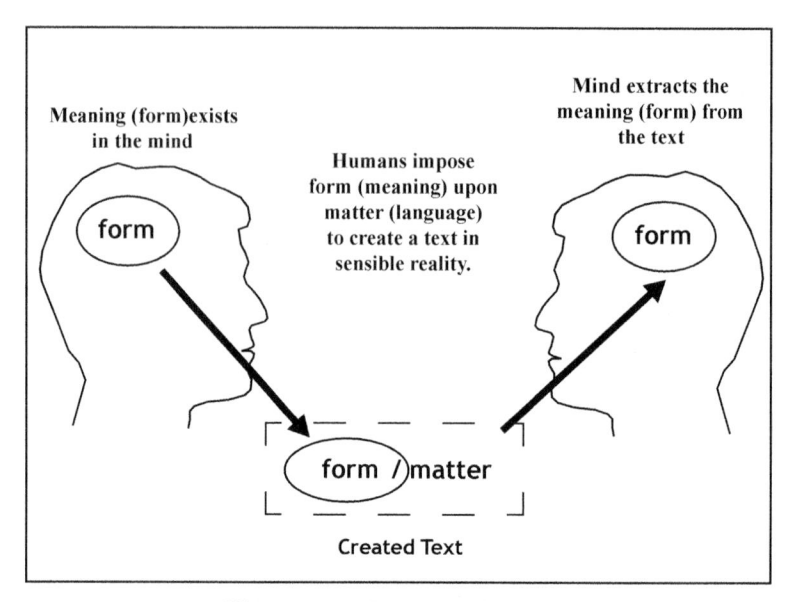

```
                    Mind extracts the
Meaning (form)exists          meaning (form) from
   in the mind                     the text
                Humans impose
                form (meaning) upon
                matter (language)
      form      to create a text in          form
                sensible reality.



                    form / matter

                    Created Text
```

Figure 12.1 Process of Knowing

writer's ideas are the exemplar cause of its meaning. The laws of thought are the instrumental cause of its meaning and the writer's purpose is the final cause of its meaning.

How do we Know a Text?

We come to know a text the same way we come to know any other finite thing that has being in sensible reality.[2] This process of knowing, explained in chapter 8, can be applied to the creation and ultimate interpretation of any text. Meaning exists as form (spiritually) in the mind of the author. The author causes a text to exist by imposing form (meaning) upon language (combining it with matter) to create a text in sensible reality (e.g., writing). The mind of the reader or hearer then extracts the form (meaning) from the text in reality. In this way a reader is able to know the meaning that is in the text (Figure 12.1).[3]

There are important principles to be applied when interpreting

---

2. As such, this understanding is not subject to the criticism leveled at justified true belief see Edmund L. Gettier, "Is Justified True Belief Knowledge?" *Analysis* 23 (1963): 212–123.

3. Adapted from Thomas A. Howe, *Towards A Thomistic Theory of Meaning* (Charlotte: Southern Evangelical Seminary, n.d.), 48.

any given text; when properly used, they help us discover the objective meaning. As Thomas Howe observes,

> The nature of reality and of the mind insures that all minds abstract according to the same principles. The individualized and universalized forms in the minds of each individual are precisely the same because they are determined by the thing in reality, not by the minds of the knowers. Consequently, meaning is grounded in being and is objectively verifiable.[4]

Interpretative principles are not arbitrary or subjective but grounded in reality since our language and its grammatical construction is used to describe reality such as persons, places, things (nouns) and actions/relationships (verbs). Out of this we derive interpretive principles and the historical grammatical method to understanding any text. For example, every text comes to us in a certain historical context as opposed to another. Knowing the context helps to discover many things about a text that aid interpretation. Who wrote it, when, where, how and sometimes why a text was created are important. The subject and genre (type of literature) and grammar are also important. The more we known about these areas the more we know about how to interpret a text. It is also important to look for the meaning in the text. We are unable to examine the mind of an author. Even if we could speak to an author, they would only be able to give us another text to interpret. So the meaning we have access to is in the text. It is not in the reader's mind or beyond the text somewhere. Furthermore, the meaning is in what is affirmed or denied by the text, not what it may or may not imply. Human language is therefore adequate to convey meaning even from God and we can properly arrive at an objective interpretation.

Hence we conclude that human language is adequate to convey meaning and humans are capable of understanding since there are principles taken from a common objectively known reality that guide us.

---

4. Thomas A. Howe, *Objectivity in Biblical Interpretation* (Advantage, 2004), 430.

Questions to Answer
1. Explain the role of objectivity in interpretation.
2. What is the role of presuppositions/preunderstanding in conflicting interpretations?
3. How do universal principles support objectivity in interpretation?
4. Apply the six different kinds of causes to a written text.

Terms and Concepts to know:
Hermeneutics
Presuposition/Preunderstanding
Objectivity
Perspective
Truth
Human Nature
Efficient cause
Final cause
Formal cause
Material cause
Exemplar cause
Instrumental cause
Meaning
Form
Matter
Historical Grammatical Method

Select Readings
Geisler, Norman L. *Systematic Theology*, Vol. 1, chap. 10.
Howe, Thomas A. *Objectivity in Biblical Interpretation.*

13 Is History Knowable?

Objectives
1. Defend the knowability of history.
2. Identify the sources and procedures for writing history.

Is History Knowable?

History is the study of the past to discover what has taken place. Historiography is the task of the historian by which he constructs a written text about the past based on evidence. The study of the past is an essential aspect of theology. The Bible claims God has intervened in human history. If this is undiscoverable or unknowable, then there is no way to discover truth about God's activities in the past. Even if the knowability of history is possible, we must still use proper methods for discovering it.

Our question regarding the knowability of history is really the same battle between relativism and objectivity. The relativist may claim, "Historical statements or claims about the past are not objectively true or knowable." Either the statement is true or it is false. If it is true, then it is a statement (made in the past) that claims to apply to all historical statements. Hence it is self–defeating. If it is false, then there is the possibility that historical statements can be objective and knowable. Since we have already established that relativism is false (see chapter 8), it is possible to assert that if a historical statement is verifiable, according to appropriate historical methods, then it is true (i.e., corresponds to reality).

Some may object by insisting that a historian, as any interpreter, brings their presuppositions and cultural influence to the task of historiography. If so it would seem that they are unable to be completely objective in their task. However, all discovery of truth, historical included, involves individual presuppositions and cultural influence. If this is the case then the issue is not whether objectivity in history is possible, but rather whose presuppositions are correct. There must be an objective ground for all statements, historical or otherwise, because, as we have shown (see chapter 10), there are universal principles that apply to everyone, including the historian. Disagreement over historical statements, presuppositions, or cultural influence should not give way to relativism.

There are some important things that make the knowability of history more likely. First, the correct world view is theistic. Since there is an absolute Mind that knows everything (past, present, and future) from eternity, history really becomes His–story. We are not saying that a historian with a different world view (e.g., Atheistic) is unable to arrive at any historical truth. We are saying, however, that because is the true world view, only a theistic historian has what is necessary in their world view to properly discover and classify events that have taken place in the past. For example, if one were to discover historical evidence for a miracle that occurred in the past. Only the theistic historian is able to properly classify and explain such an event. The atheistic historian has no way to incorporate a theistic miracle into their understanding of history. They are forced, as a result of their world view, to classify, regardless of the evidence, such an event in natural terms such as a myth, hoax, or an anomaly yet to be explained.

Second, it is important to realize the nature of history as a subject of investigation. Philosopher Mortimer J. Adler helps us in this endeavor by observing,

> On the one hand, we have self–evident truths that have certitude and incorrigibility; and we also have truths

that are still subject to doubt but that are supported by
evidence and reason to a degree that puts them beyond
reasonable doubt or at least give them predominance
over contrary views. All else is mere opinion—with no
claim to being knowledge or having any hold on truth.
. . . There is no question that the findings and conclusions of historical research are knowledge in this sense."[1]

While it is admitted that perfect absolute objectivity is only possible for an infinite mind, (i.e., God) a theistic world view does provide the proper framework for the construction of a limited (i.e., open to revision) objective construction of the past.

Third, is the importance of skill, expertise, and the well roundedness of the historian. Philosopher Jacques Maritain (1882–1973) expresses this by saying,

> For the historian it is a prerequisite that he have a sound
> philosophy of man, an integrated culture, an accurate
> appreciation of the human being's various activities and
> their comparative importance, a correct scale of moral,
> political, religious, technical and artistic values. The
> value, I mean the truth, of the historical work will be in
> proportion to the human richness of the historian.[2]

Hence, whatever history is produced, the truth or objectivity of it, will be proportionate to the correct views, experience, and method of the historian.

How History is Discovered

History usually involves the examination of various sources. These sources can be oral or written and are divided into two types: primary and secondary. According to Louis Gottschalk, "A primary source is the testimony of an eyewitness . . . A primary source must thus have been produced by a contemporary of the events it narrates. It does not, however, need to be original in the legal sense of the word original – that is, the very document (usually the first written draft) whose contents are the subject of discussion – for

---

1. Mortimer J. Adler, *Ten Philosophical Mistakes* (New York: Macmillan, 1985), 100–101.

2. Jacques Maritain, *On The Philosophy of History* (Clifton, NJ: Augustus M. Kelley, 1973), 7–8.

quite often a later copy or a printed edition will do just as well; and in the case of the Greek and Roman classics seldom are any but later copies available."[3] A secondary source "is the testimony of anyone who is not an eyewitness – that is, of one who was not present at the events of which he tells."[4]

In biblical and systematic theology an examination to discover the credibility of such sources is usually divided into two types of criticism: lower and higher. Lower criticism examines the text by using available manuscripts to comparing and contrasting them to reconstruct, as closely as possible, the original text. Higher criticism examines the content of what is said in text itself. It attempts to answer such questions about the origin of the text which includes its authorship, audience, reliability, authenticity, etc. It is at this point that a critic's world view becomes very important to the process. Critics who approach a certain text with negative or unwarranted philosophical presuppositions must be scrutinized. Any approach that rejects theism and/or miracles must be rejected. As we have seen there is no completely neutral or unbiased approach. The question is, who's bias or presupposition conforms to the true world view. Hence, prolegomena becomes extremely important. Those failing to answer such questions related to prolegomena or arriving at incorrect answers are doomed in their theology as well.

The next inquiry concerns discovering historical justification and truth based on these sources. Historical justification refers to reasons that exist for thinking a historical description is true. Historical events, names, places, and testimony that are mentioned in sources may have corroborating evidence from other sources or archeological discoveries. After the statements and descriptions of a general or specific nature can start to be made, historical truth can then be claimed. Historian C. Behan McCullagh states that "a description of the world is true if one set of its possible truth conditions does exist or has existed in reality." He gives the example; Caesar's army crossed the Rubicon. "The statement is very general but there are many ways that it could have been fulfilled. The description is true if one of the many possible sets of truth conditions

---

3. Louis Gottschalk, *Understanding History: A Primer of Historical Method* (New York: Alrfed A. Knopf, 1964), 53–54, emphasis his.

4. Ibid., 148, emphasis his.

occurred in reality."[5] The final step is to organize reliable testimony into a meaningful narrative or exposition.

Much of theology requires historical investigation in terms of events and ideas. Humans should engage in the study of the past with the theistic world view in place and a proper understanding of the nature of history. This combined with a proper methodology allows us to know and speak of historical truth given the support of extant evidence.

Questions to Answer
1. Explain why a theistic world view is important for one to properly do historiography?
2. Why is history knowable?

Terms and Concepts to know:
History
Historiography
Presupposition
Objectivity
Primary source
Secondary source
Lower criticism
Higher criticism

Select Readings
Geisler, Norman L. *Christian Apologetics*, chap. 17.
McDowell, Josh. *The New Evidence that Demands a Verdict*, chap. 40.

---

5. C. Behan McCullagh, *Justifying Historical Descriptions* (New York: Cambridge University Press, 1984), 8.

SECTION FOUR
Theological Methodology

There are three basic prerequisites to revelation: 1) A Being capable of giving it; 2) A being capable of receiving it; 3) A medium through which it can be given (rational thought, meaning, truth, analogy, etc.). The preceding chapters have attempted to legitimize these prerequisites. There is an unchanging absolutely perfect Being (God) that can communicate an error free message that expresses absolute truth and meaning which can be interpreted, understood and objectively known by finite human beings.

The final section deals with the nature of God's revelation and the methodology (chapter 14) one should use to arrive at a systematic theology.

14 How to Do Systematic Theology

Objectives
1. Distinguish between general and special revelation.
2. Define the steps for doing systematic theology in order.

God's Revelation

Evangelical theology holds that Revelation can be found in two spheres: 1) Nature and 2) Scripture. Romans 1:19–20 speaks of the former:

> Because that which is known about God is evident within them; for God made it evident to them. For since the creation of the world His invisible attributes, His eternal power and divine nature, have been clearly seen, being understood through what has been made, so that they are without excuse.

Second Timothy 3:16–17 speaks of the later saying:

> All Scripture is inspired by God and profitable for teaching, for reproof, for correction, for training in righteousness; so that the man of God may be adequate, equipped for every good work.

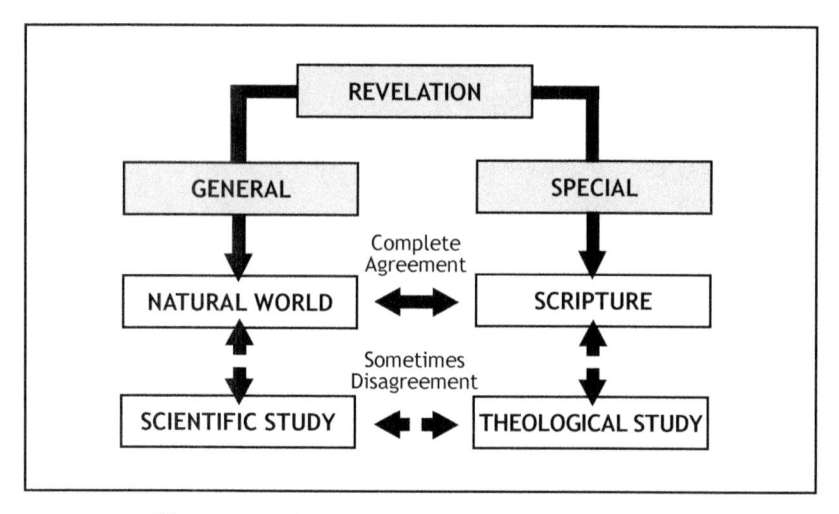

Figure 14.1 Revelation: General and Special

Romans 1:19–20 speaks of what is theologically called general revelation and 2 Tim. 3:16–17 speaks of special revelation. Human reasoning can show that general revelation is possible since it can demonstrate the existence and nature of God, finite beings that can receive and understand it, and the possibility of objective meaning and truth. However, it is special revelation found only in the canonical books of Scripture that actually manifest the reality of God's specific message, in human language, to human beings. It is only here that we learn God is a Trinity (Tri–unity), the plan of redemption, and the savior Jesus Christ. General revelation is to all humans, but special revelation is specifically for believers. General revelation contains truth and morality available to all humankind, but special revelation contains truth and morality specifically to God's people. General revelation is sufficient to condemn humans, but only special revelation contains the message and means of salvation.

Special revelation consists of the sixty six books recognized as Scripture. What identifies these books as Scripture concerns the rule, standard or canon applied to discover what books constitute special revelation. Norman Geisler's *General Introduction to the Bible* lists and applies the following general principles in discovering the canon of Scripture.

1. Written by a prophet of God (Heb. 1:1; 2 Pet. 1:20–21)
2. Confirmed by an act of God (Heb. 2:3–4; John 3:2; Acts 2:22)
3. Tell the truth about God (Deut. 6:22f.; Gal. 1:8)
4. Has the power of God (Heb. 4:12)
5. Accepted by the people of God (1 Thess. 2:13; Dan. 9:2; 2 Pet. 3:15)

Such rules or standards while reflected in Scripture are grounded in theological prolegomena. The first is supported by the fact that humans can receive a message from God (chapter 7) since human language is adequate to convey meaning (chapter 11), be preserved in a text and interpreted (chapter 12) by others. The second is a message and messenger that can be confirmed by an identifiable act of God (chapter 6). The third is a message that can tell the truth, as opposed to what is false, about God (chapters 8–9, 11). The fourth is again the power of God (chapter 6) which can be detected along with the fifth via a study of history which is knowable (chapter 13). Such a grounding of the principles is important to establishing the basis upon which the canon is recognized. As such the principles themselves are not circular or dependent upon any one human council, creed or individual's acceptance or rejection of the canonical books (Figure 14.2).

Because the nature of God is perfect, infallible, and unable to error (inerrant), it follows that all of God's revelation must also be,

Principle of Canonicity	Basis in Prolegomena
1. Written by a prophet of God	• Does the Christian God exist? • What is man that he can know? • Can we talk about God?
2. Confirmed by an act of God	• Does the Christian God exist? • Are miracles real?
3. Tell the truth about God	• What is truth? • Can we talk about God?
4. Has the power of God	• Does the Christian God exist? • Are miracles real?
5. Accepted by the people of God	• Is history knowable? • Is an objective interpretation possible?

Figure 14.2 Test for Canonicity

in its original state, infallible and inerrant. Hence, both special and general revelation, because they have the same infallible and inerrant source (i.e., God) must be in complete agreement and without error. The natural world and written Scripture have the same creator/author. Therefore, they must agree. This, however, does not preclude fallible humans from misunderstanding or incorrectly interpreting the natural world or Scripture. But such conflicts exist in the understanding or interpretation between humans; they do not exist between the facts of the natural world and Scripture themselves. The natural world is discovered through scientific study and the Scriptures are discovered by theological study.

As we have stated systematic theology, to be complete, must inquire into other fields of study relevant to general revelation. As one systematic theology states,

> In theology the interaction between biblical studies and other disciplines should always be a two–way street. No one provides a monologue for the other; all engage in continual dialogue. Although the Bible is infallible in whatever it addresses, it does not speak to every issue. Furthermore, . . . while the Bible is infallible, our interpretation of it is not. Thus, those in biblical studies must listen to as well as speak to the other disciplines. Only in this way can a complete and correct systematic world view be construction.[1]

The subjects of science and theology, because they are endeavors of human beings, are subject to human error. As we have said, it is important to understand such error is not attributable to God; it always is the result of human limitations or error. But it is valid to ask, in such cases of conflict, which revelation is to be given priority in an attempt to settle a disagreement. While we might be tempted to say we should put the Bible first, it should be kept in mind that human interpretation of the infallible word is subject to human fallible misunderstanding. This is also true for the history of science.[2] Priority then should go to the interpretation or understanding that is more clear and certain. While understanding that

---

1. Norman Geisler, *Introduction Bible,* Vol. 1. *Systematic Theology* (Minneapolis: Bethany House, 2002), 79.

2. See Nigel Brush, *The Limitations of Scientific Truth* (Grand Rapids: Kregel, 2005).

revisions may have to be made when new evidence either in science or theology becomes available.

For example consider some clearly false interpretations of the Bible that have historically been held by some. That the Earth is flat according to Rev. 7:1 which says it has four corners. Both science and a proper understanding of the genre of apocalyptic literature have corrected this miss–understanding. In Joshua 1:15 it states that the Sun rises (moves around the earth). Yet, this need not imply, as some have understood it, that the Sun must move around the earth. Instead, this is observational or phenomenal language frequently used even today since it describes what is observed and not what is actually the case. There are also some clear false understandings in science to consider. The naturalistic theory of evolution, for example, asserts that all the different variety of living organism is the result of macro evolutionary change. However, the Bible clearly asserts that each was created after its kind and humans are in the image of God (Gen. 1:21; 27). One scientific problem is that there is no adequate mechanism put forth to account for such change,[3] and there is a clear understanding of the scriptural statements and meaning. Hence, priority must be given to Scripture because of its clearer teaching.

It is also worth noting that there are other areas where we currently may not have enough evidence or grasp of the issue from either a scientific or theological position. In such cases we may not be able to speak with certainty on questions related to nature and Scripture. One example of this may be the length of time involved in God's creation. Theologians disagree with each other on the specific interpretation of the word "day" in Genesis chapters 1 and 2.

Method of Systematic Theology

The goal of systematic theology is to present as completely

---

3. Natural selection is put forth as this mechanism, however, this presupposes a replicating system and the only evidence for the biological component of this theory remains micro evolution (genetic changes within species) which has never empirically been observed, tested, or adequately explained at the macro evolutionary (changes between species) level. See Walter L. Bradley and Charles B. Thaxton, "Information and the Origin of Life" in J. P. Moreland, ed. *The Creation Hypothesis* (Wheaton: InterVarsity Press, 1994), 173–210.

as possible a comprehensive understanding of all God's revelation (general and special). To accomplish this one must employ a method. Assumed in this method, is that the theologian has done a prolegomena. Failure to do this properly affects the method and any theology produced. Six steps will be explained to understand the process of doing systematic theology. They will be integrated with the doctrine of inerrancy to fully demonstrate how they apply to the development of a specific theological doctrine. The six steps include the following: 1) Inductive Study; 2) Deductive Conclusion; 3) Retroduction; 4) Abduction; 5) Systematic Correlation; and 6) Practical Application. See Figure 14.3.[4]

1) Inductive Study. The first step is that of inductively studying all scriptural passages related to the doctrine. The procedure is to exegete all scriptural texts that are relevant to the development of a specific doctrine. The process must adhere to the rules of hermeneutics and employ the literal–historical–grammatical method of interpretation. The end product is the biblical basis for the specific doctrine. For example, our doctrine of inerrancy reveals at least two central and relevant texts: Hebrews 6:18 says "it is impossible for God to lie" (cf. Titus 1:2). Second Timothy 3:16 says "All Scripture is inspired by God." An inductive study of these texts gives us the result that God cannot err and that the Scripture is God's word. What we have explained, up to this point, is the biblical basis for the doctrine of inerrancy.

2) Deductive Conclusion. The second step is to draw a deductive conclusion based on our inductive study of all relevant doctrines in the first step. The result is the following:

> 1) It is impossible for God to err.
> 2) The Bible is the word of God.
> 3) Therefore, it is impossible for the Bible to err.

This method is tested by the laws of logic. For example, there are no formal fallacies in the above deductive argument, so it is valid. Our premises have material correspondence to the facts of Scripture established in the first step. Hence, we have explained the logical validity of inerrancy.

---

4. Adapted from Geisler, *Prolegomena*, Class Notes.

3) Retroduction. Retroduction is similar to induction, but it allows us to take a look (or re–look) at other information and data outside our premises that is known or assumed to be related. In the doctrine of inerrancy, retroduction allows us to examine any other scriptural data, any other doctrines in Scripture, other facts that would be found in the world, and to draw any analogies between the world and Scripture. For example some things we would discover about the Bible in our retroduction step are that the original manuscripts, called autographs, no longer exist. All that exists are hand written copies of manuscripts and it is clear that these contain some errors. Furthermore, these copies clearly reflect human literary forms and reflect the current culture at the time of writing. It is at this stage that we may also take into account facts found in general revelation. This may include facts about God or the created world. The nature of God known from our argument also informs us that He is perfect and without error. We may also learn information from the study of science that demonstrates that the world is not flat or square. Such information is relevant to the study of Scripture and the formation of the doctrine of inerrancy, since we will want to interpret Scripture and formulate our doctrines so as not to conflict with known facts of the world. Retroduction is tested by our abilities to be comprehensive, consistent, and adequate in our assessment of the data. If we are, then we will have explained the factual basis of inerrancy.

4) Abduction. Abduction is the reasoning process that works in the reverse order of deduction. It allows us to step outside of our deductive argument that says a entails b and ask if instead there is any other evidence or reason for b. It allows us to take what we learned from the retroductive stage and qualify and strengthen our previous conclusion. This process gives us insight to the data collected during retroduction and may yield a conceptual model to help our explanation of the conclusion. The result is a qualified conclusion that incorporates additional information found through reduction. Hence, we can further include in our understanding of inerrancy that it must include both a human and divine element. That it must only apply to the originals, since some copies do contain known errors. It must also be properly understood in terms of the culture of when it was written. Such a process is tested by our insightfulness and creativity. It helps explain the doctrine more fully in terms of its human and divine origin. In the process of abduction we may also find some helpful analogies with other doctrines. A helpful one concerning inerrancy is between Christ and the Bible. Christ was without sin, and the Bible is without error. As with all analogies, however, there are limitations and areas of disagreement. After all they would not be analogies if they were completely the same. But they may nonetheless be helpful in understanding some concepts.

5) Systematic Correlation. Systematic Correlation is the step that attempts to correlate results of the study and express it in a systematic manner. The method uses all the previous tests. The result should be a systematic explanation of the doctrinal study. With the example of inerrancy we may say, "The Bible is God's inerrant word in the original manuscripts in terms of culture and literary forms of its day." If these steps 1–5 are done with every doctrine presented in Scripture, then the result at this stage is a written systematic theology.

6) Practical Application. The final step is to explain the doctrinal application to the Christian life. This may be referred to as its practical or livability stage. It answers the questions what difference does the doctrine make when it comes to thinking about and living the Christian life? The procedure is to show what obedience is expected or can come from someone believing the doctrine. The result is hopefully a transformed life. It can be tested by the good works produced or fruit of the spirit evident in the believer's life. When this step is completed it has explained the practical applicability of Christian doctrine to the life of the believer. A believer who holds to the doctrine of inerrancy will hopefully gain confidence and trust in God, who is incapable of error and that the Bible is trustworthy in all respect. The believer can confidently read the word of God, trust God, do what Scripture commands, and live a faithful and fruitful Christian life.

To be systematic in theology we must not only study the relevant passages of Scripture (inductive), make rational arguments from Scripture (deductive), but incorporate truths found in other disciplines such as biblical and historical theology, science, philosophy and wherever God's truth may be found (retroduction). We must reason through this material and develop creative models of integration (abduction). Then a systematic correlation can be written with practical application. The result will be a human synthesis of all of God's revelation both general and special.

Questions to Answer

1. Explain what can be known from general and special revelation.
2. Explain why general and special revelation must agree and how to approach the problem of disagreements.
3. List and define each step in the methodology of doing systematic theology.
4. Choose a doctrine of Scripture and follow each step of the methodology to briefly outline the method behind the systematic expression of that doctrine (use Figure 14.3).

Terms and Concepts to know:

General Revelation
Special Revelation
Inductive Study
Deductive Conclusion
Retroduction
Abduction
Systematic Correlation
Practical (Livability)

Select Readings

Geisler, Norman L. *Systematic Theology*, Vol. 1, chap. 12.
Geisler, Norman L., ed. *Inerrancy*.

122 A Prolegomena to Evangelical Theology

Methodology	Procedure	Results	Tested By	What is Explained
1. Inductive study [of all doctrine(s)]	Exegesis (of all relevant texts)	1. God cannot err 2. Bible is God's word	Hermeneutical principles	Biblical basis of inerrancy
2. Deductive conclusion (from doctrine)	Deductive (of another doctrine)	3. Therefore, Bible cannot err	2. Logical laws	Logical validity of inerrancy
3. Retroductive use of a. Data of Scripture b. Other doctrines of Scripture c. Other facts in the world d. analogies in nature and Scripture	Critical and comparative study of a. Data of Scripture b. Other Doctrines of Scripture c. Relevant facts of General Revelation	4. Originals are unavailable 5. Some actual contradictions and errors in available texts 6. Human literary forms are used 7. Culture of the day is reflected 8. Fact: earth is not flat or square. 9. Analogy of Christ and Bible: both are flawless	3. Comprehensive 4. Consistency 5. Adequacy	Factual basis of inerrancy
4. Abductive	Insight (develop model)	10. Hence, inerrancy means Bible is: a. both human and divine b. yet without error in originals c. As experienced in culture of the day	1–5 above 6. Creativity (insightfulness)	Source (origin) of inerrancy doctrine
5. Systematic Correlation	Systematize under Results 1–10	11. Bible is God's inerrant word in original manuscripts in terms of culture and literary forms of its day	1–6 above	Theological understanding of inerrancy
6. Practical (Livability)	Obedience	12. Transformed life	7. Fruit of the Spirit (good works)	Practical Applicability

Figure 14.3 Methodology

APPENDIX: Faith and Reason

There are two extremes with respect to this issue: rationalism and fideism. Rationalism holds that one can determine by rational means all truth about God, leaving no room for faith. Fideism holds one must blindly believe without any rational thought or evidence. This being the case, a middle ground must be carved out between these extremes.

Aquinas shows that faith and reason are distinct but complimentary human capacities or habits of the soul. Both Augustine and Aquinas agree that faith is a virtue by which things not seen are believed based on authority.[1] Aquinas elaborates,

> Whatever things we know with scientific knowledge properly so called we know by reducing them to first

---

1. This is compatible with Hebrews 11:1 and although he employs different terminology, it is not different from John Calvin's understanding of faith and reason, see Arvin Vos, *Aquinas, Calvin & Contemporary Protestant Thought* (Grand Rapids: Christian University Press, 1985), chapter 1.

> principles which are naturally present to the understanding. In this way all scientific knowledge terminates in the sight of a thing which is present. Hence, it is impossible to have faith and scientific knowledge about the same thing."[2]

The object of faith is unseen while the object of the sciences, which includes philosophical demonstration, is seen. For example, the Trinity is beyond all human capacity to demonstrate its truth and is therefore accepted on the authority of God's revelation. While the existence of God, because it can be demonstrated, for those who can understand such demonstration it is not by faith, it is by reason.

Furthermore, faith is often more certain than reason because reason is limited. It is limited in terms of its subject which may be beyond sense experience (i.e., God) or even the power of human reason. It is also limited in terms of some who lack the intellectual effort or time to pursue it. Reason can also be affected or repressed by sin. While it can be said that sin affects human reason it cannot be possible that sin completely destroys human rationality, for not only would we be unable to reason about that truth we would also no longer be able to sin. Aquinas says,

> The good of nature, that is diminished by sin, is the natural inclination to virtue, which is befitting to man from the very fact that he is a rational being; for it is due to this that he performs actions in accord with reason, which is to act virtuously. Now sin cannot entirely take away from man the fact that he is a rational being, for then he would no longer be capable of sin. Wherefore it is not possible for this good of nature to be destroyed entirely.[3]

Faith is personal trust in someone based on their authority because we do not have complete or direct understanding of the matter. In some cases we may question or not be certain about the authority which may lead to doubt or opinion, since again, we do not know the matter directly. But faith can also be certain or without doubting the authority, because it is the inner act of believing, that produces faith which is rooted in our will rather than our intellect

---

2. Thomas Aquinas, *Truth* XIV, 9, reply.
3. Thomas Aquinas, *Summa Theologica* 1a2ae. 85, 2.

	Before Faith	Act of Faith	After Faith
Reasoning	Mind	Present but never basis/cause	Present but never basis/cause
Faith	No believing *in*	Believing *in*	Believing *in*
Basis	Reason *that*	Faith/Authority	Faith/Authority
Cause of consent	Intellect	Will	Intellect & Will

Figure A.1 Faith and Reason

or reason. Hence, having faith may lead the intellect to search, ponder and reason about its object, but there is a firm assent to its authority. Reason, on the other hand, involves our own ability or intellect to demonstrate and understand that something is true. Faith is primarily an act of the will that trusts in an authoritative source. As such, faith is not contrary to reason and reason cannot force faith since it is rooted in the will, not the intellect.

Reason is present before, during, and after believing. However, reason alone cannot bring us to faith in God. Faith can never cause or be based on reason. If it were based on reason then faith would not be a free act of the will. Consent would be directly caused by the mind alone. But because it is possible for some to intellectually assent to truth but not have faith, the two faculties must be distinct. At best faith can only be supported or be influenced by reason. A good illustration of this is marriage. One may meet many who they reason *that* they would be a good spouse. Yet only to the beloved one do they say "I will" to be *in* marriage.

Thus, reason and evidence are never coercive of faith. Norman Geisler observes, "Reason can be used to demonstrate that God exists, but it can never in itself persuade someone to believe in God. Only God can do this, working by his grace in and through free choice."[4] Reason involves the mind (by rational means) coming to the conclusion that something is true while faith involves the will (by faith only influenced or supported by reason) coming to the conviction to believe in something. In short, the distinction is between believing *that* something is true and believing *in* something. The former involves the intellect, while the latter involves the will or volitional capacity of humans.

---

4. Norman L. Geisler, *Thomas Aquinas* (Grand Rapids: Baker, 1991), 69.

BIBLIOGRAPHY

Adler, Mortimer J. *Ten Philosophical Mistakes*. New York: Macmillan, 1985.

———. *Intellect: Mind over Matter*. New York: Macmillan, 1990.

Aquinas, Thomas. *Compendium of Theology*. St. Louis: B. Herder Book, 1948.

———. *Summa Contra Gentiles*. Vols. 1–5. Translated by Anton C. Pegis. London: Notre Dame Press, 1975.

———. *Summa Theologica*. Vols. 1–5. Translated by English Dominican Province. Allen, TX: Christian Classics, 1981.

———. *Truth*. Vols. 1–3. Translated by James V. McGlynn. Indianapolis: Hackett Pub., 1994.

Aristotle. *The Complete Works of Aristotle*. Edited by J. Barnes. 2 vols. Princeton, NJ: Princeton University Press, 1984.

Barber, Cyril J. and Robert M. Krauss. *An Introduction to Theological Research*. Washington, D.C.: University Press of America, 2000.

Behe, Michael J. *Darwin's Black Box: The Biochemical Challenge to Evolution*. New York: The Free Press, 1996.

Bloom, Allen. *The Closing of the American Mind*. New York: Simon and Schuster, 1988.

Bromiley, Geoffrey W. *Historical Theology: An Introduction*. Grand Rapids, Eerdmans, 1978.

Brush, Nigel. *The Limitations of Scientific Truth*. Grand Rapids: Kregel, 2005.

Chafer, Lewis Sperry. *Systematic Theology*. 2 Vols. Abridged Edition. Edited by John F. Walvoord. Wheaton: Victor Books, 1988.

Corduan, Winfried. *Handmaid to Theology: An Essay in Philosophical Prolegomena*. Grand Rapids: Baker Books, 1981.

Craig, William Lane. *Reasonable Faith: Christian Truth and Apologetics*. 3rd ed. Wheaton: Crossway Books, 2008.

———. *The Kalām Cosmological Argument*. New York: Macmillan, 1979.

Davies, Brian. *The Reality of God and the Problem of Evil*. New York: Coninuum, 2006.

———. *The Thought of Thomas Aquinas*. Oxford: Oxford University Press, 1993.

Descartes, Rená. *Descartes Selected Philosophical Writings*. Translated by John Cottingham, et al. New York: Cambridge University Press, 1994.

DeWolf, Harold L. *The Case for Theology in Liberal Perspective*. Philadelphia: Westminster, 1959.

Elwell, Walter A., ed. *Topical Analysis of the Bible*. Grand Rapids: Baker Book House, 1991.

Enns, Paul. *The Moody Handbook of Theology*. Chicago: Moody Press, 1989.

Feser, Edward. *Aquinas: A Beginner's Guide*. Oxford: Oneworld Pub., 2009.

Geisler, Norman L. *Baker Encyclopedia of Apologetics*. Grand Rapids: Baker Books, 1999.

———. *Christian Apologetics*. 2nd ed. Grand Rapids, Baker Books, 2013.

———. *Creating God in the Image of Man?* Minneapolis: Bethany House, 1997.

———. *Chosen But Free*. 3rd ed. Minneapolis: Bethany House, 2010.

———. *If God Why Evil?* Minneapolis: Bethany House, 2011.

———. ed. *Inerrancy*. Grand Rapids: Zondervan, 1980.

———. *Miracles and the Modern Mind*. Grand Rapids: Baker, 1992.

———. *Signs and Wonders*. Wheaton: Tyndale House, 1988.

———. *Systematic Theology*. Vol. 1–4. Eugene: Bethany House, 2002–2004.

———. *Twelve Points The Show Christianity is True*. Indian Trail: NGIM, 2015.

———. *Thomas Aquinas: An Evangelical Appraisal*. Grand Rapids: Baker, 1991.

———. "Religious Pluralism: A Christian Response" *Christian Apologetics Journal*, Vol. 4, no. 2 Fall 2005, 1–27.

———. "The Concept of Truth in the Inerrancy Debate" *Bibliotheca Sacra*, vol 137, no. 548, Oct.–Dec. 1980, 327–339.

Geisler, Norman L. and Douglas E. Potter. *A Popular Survey of Bible Doctrine*. Indian Trail: NGIM, 2015.

Geisler, Norman L. and Paul D. Feinberg. *Introduction to Philosophy: A Christian Perspective*. Grand Rapids: Baker Books, 1987.

Geisler, Norman L. and Ronald Brooks. *Come Let Us Reason*. Grand Rapids: Baker, 1990.

Geisler, Norman L. and William Watkins. *Worlds Apart*. Grand Rapids: Baker, 1989.

Geisler, Norman L. and William E. Nix. *General Introduction to the Bible*. Rev. and exp. Chicago: Moody Press, 1986.

Geisler, Norman and Winfried Corduan. *Philosophy of Religion*, 2nd ed. Grand Rapids, Baker Books, 1988.

Gilson, Etienne. *Methodical Realism*. Front Royal: Christendom Press, 1990.

———. *Thomistic Realism and The Critique of Knowledge*. Translated by Mark A. Wauck. San Francisco: Ignatius Press, 1986.

Gettier, Edmund L. "Is Justified True Belief Knowledge?" *Analysis* 23 (1963): 212–123.

Gottschalk, Louis. *Understanding History: A Primer of Historical Method*. New York: Alrfed A. Knopf, 1964.

Hackett, Stuart C. *The Resurrection of Theism*. 2nd ed. Grand Rapids: Baker Books, 1982.

Hick, John. *A Christian Theology of Religions*. Louisville: Westminster John Knox Press, 1995.

Howe, Richard Glenn. "An Analysis of William Lane Craig's Kalam Cosmological Argument." Master's thesis, University of Mississippi, 1990.

Howe, Thomas A. "Hermeneutics and Metaphysics" *Christian Apologetics Journal*, Vol. 3, no. 2 Fall 2004, 1–11.

———. *Objectivity in Biblical Interpretation*. Altamonte Springs: Advantage Books, 2003.

———. "Practical Hermeneutics: How to Interpret Your Bible Correctly (Part Two)," *Christian Research Journal* 25 (2003).

———. *Towards A Thomistic Theory of Meaning*. Charlotte: Southern Evangelical Seminary, n.d.

Hume, David. *Enquiries Concerning Human Understanding and Concerning the Principles of Morals,* 3d. ed. New York: Clarendon Press, 1992.

Kant, Immanuel. *Critique of Pure Reason*. Translated by. Werner S. Pluhar. Indianapolis: Hackett, 1996.

Kreeft, Peter. S*ocratic Logic: A Logic Text using Socratic Method, Platonic Questions, and Aristotelian Principles*, 3.1. ed. St. Augustines Press, 2010.

Lewis, C. S. *Mere Christianity*. New York: Macmillan, 1952.

———. *The Abolition of Man*. New York: MacMillan, 1947.

Maritain, Jacques. *On the Philosophy of History*. Clifton, NJ: Kelley, 1973.

McCullagh, C. Behan. *Justifying Historical Descriptions*. New York: Cambridge University Press, 1984.

McDowell, Josh. *The New Evidence that Demands a Verdict,* Nashville: Thomas Nelson, 1999.

McInerny, Ralph. *A First Glance at St. Thomas Aquinas: A Handbook for Peeping Thomists.* Notre Dame: University of Notre Dame Press, 1990.

Moreland, J. P., ed. *The Creation Hypothesis*. Wheaton: InterVarsity Press, 1994.

Paley, William. *Natural Theology.* New York: Oxford University Press, 2008.

Pinnock, Clark, et al. *The Openness of God: A Biblical Challenge to the Traditional Understanding of God*. Downers Grove, InterVarsity Press, 1994.

Potter, Douglas E. *Developing a Christian Apologetics Educational Program: In the Secondary School*. Eugene: Wipf & Stock, 2010.

Ryrie, Charles C. *Basic Theology: A Popular Systematic Guide to Understanding Biblical Truth*. Chicago: Moody Press, 1999.

———. *Biblical Theology of the New Testament*. Chicago, Moody Press, 1959.

Schaff, Philip. *Post–Nicene Fathers*. 14 vols. 1st Series Reprint 1887, Peabody: Hendrickson, 1999.

Sorley, W. R. *Moral Values and the Idea of God.* London: Cambridge University Press, 1918.

Spinoza, Beneditc de. *A Theologico–Political Treatise and A Political Treatise*, Translated by R. H. M. Elwes. New York Dover, 1951.

Taylor, Richard. *Metaphysics*, 4th ed. Englewood Cliffs: Prentice Hall, 1992.

Veatch, Henry B. "St. Thomas and the Question, 'How Are Synthetic Judgment's *A Priori* Possible?'" *The Modern Schoolman* 42 (March 1965): 239–263.

Vos, Arvin. *Aquinas, Calvin & Contemporary Protestant Thought*. Grand Rapids: Christian University Press, 1985.

Warfield, Benjamin B. *The Idea of Systematic Theology*, Vol. 9, *The Works of Benjamin B. Warfield*. Oxford 1932. Reprint Grand Rapids: Baker Books, 2003.

Wilhelmsen, Frederick D. *Man's Knowledge of Reality: An Introduction to Thomistic Epistemology*. Englewood Cliffs: Prentice–Hall, 1956.

Yockey, Hubert. *Information Theory and Molecular Biology*. Cambridge: Cambridge University Press, 1992.

NGIM
NORM GEISLER INTERNATIONAL MINISTRIES

Norm Geisler International Ministries is dedicated to carrying on the life's work of its co-founder, Norman L. Geisler. Described as a cross between Billy Graham and Thomas Aquinas, Norm Geisler, PhD, is a prolific author, professor, apologist, philosopher, and theologian. He has authored or co-authored over 100 books and co-founded 2 seminaries.

NGIM is focused on equipping others to proclaim and defend the Christian Faith by providing evangelism and apologetic training.

More Information

Website:	http://NormGeisler.com
Training:	http://NGIM.org (Norm Geisler International Ministries)
e–Books:	http://BastionBooks.com
Email:	Dr.NormanGeisler@outlook.com
Facebook:	http://facebook.com/normgeisler
Twitter:	https://www.twitter.com/normgeisler
Videos:	http://www.youtube.com/user/DrNormanLGeisler/videos
Biblical Inerrancy:	http://DefendingInerrancy.com

Printed in Great Britain
by Amazon